DISCIPLE

FAST TRACK

Becoming Disciples Through Bible Study

NEW TESTAMENT
STUDY MANUAL

DISCIPLE FAST TRACK
New Testament Study Manual
Copyright © 2016 by Abingdon Press
DISCIPLE: BECOMING DISCIPLES THROUGH BIBLE STUDY
Study Manual, copyright © 1987 by Graded Press
Second Edition, copyright © 1993 by Abingdon Press
All rights reserved.

Writers: Richard Byrd Wilke and Julia Kitchens Wilke
New Testament Consultant to the Writers: Leander E. Keck
General Editor: Susan Wilke Fuquay
Design Manager and Illustrator: Keely Moore

19 20 21 22 23 24 25 — 10 9 8 7
Manufactured in the United States of America

DISCIPLE FAST TRACK

CONTENTS

As You Begin DISCIPLE FAST TRACK

You are committing yourself to at least three to four hours a week of independent study and preparation, plus seventy-five minutes each week in the weekly group meeting, for twenty-four weeks when you complete both the Old Testament and New Testament studies.

To establish a disciplined pattern of study, choose and stick to a particular time and location for daily reading and writing, study, reflection, and prayer.

Choosing a Bible

This Study Manual is based on the Common English Bible. We recommend *The CEB Study Bible: with Apocrypha*, edited by Joel B. Green (Common English Bible, 2013). Other excellent study Bibles and translations are available. Keep one or two handy for comparing difficult verses or passages.

Study Manual Format

This Study Manual is a discipline. It is a plan to guide your private study and preparation for the weekly group meeting.

Common elements appear throughout the lessons. The theme word, Scripture verse(s), and title at the beginning of each lesson suggest the subject and direction of the lesson. Together, they can help you remember the sequence of the biblical story.

"Our Human Condition" expresses a common human experience and provides a perspective from which to read and listen to Scripture.

Daily Bible reading assignments are listed and space is provided for making notes about the Scripture—key ideas, persons, events, new insights, geographic or historic information, the meaning of particular words, and questions you have about the Scripture that you want to raise in the group meeting.

Daily assignments also indicate when to read and respond to "The Bible Teaching" and the "Marks of Discipleship" sections of the lesson. The day on which you do this work will vary depending on the content of the lesson. The "Marks of Discipleship" identify particular characteristics of disciples and invite you to think about ways your life and the life of your congregation reflect those characteristics. Don't rush through this part of your work. It will be a valuable source of insight and discussion for you and members of the group.

"If You Want to Know More" suggests additional individual reading and study and the occasional preparation of a report to the group. The additional study resources suggested below will be helpful here.

As you begin your daily study, use the prayer psalm from the "Prayer" section. Write down concerns about which you will pray during the week.

Additional Study Resources

Though you need only the Bible and this Study Manual for successful study of DISCIPLE FAST TRACK, these reference books will help you go deeper into study of the Scriptures:

- *The CEB Bible: Bible Dictionary* (Common English Bible, Nashville, 2011)
- *The CEB Concise Concordance* (Common English Bible, 2012)
- *CEB Bible Map Guide* (Common English Bible, 2011)

How to Get the Most From Reading Scripture

- Read with curiosity. Ask the questions *who, what, where, when, how,* and *why* as you read.
- Learn as much as you can about the passage you are studying. It will help you hear God speak to you through the Scripture. Try to discover what the writer was saying for the time in which the passage was written. Read the surrounding verses and chapters to establish the setting or situation in which the action or teaching took place.
- Pay attention to the form of the passage, because meaning exists not only in what is said but in the form in which it is said. How you read and understand poetry or a parable will differ from how you read and understand historical narrative.
- Don't force your interpretation on the biblical text. Let the Scripture speak for itself.
- Question the Scripture, but also learn to read Scripture so you find answers to your questions in the Scripture itself. The biblical text will solve some of the problems you have with a particular passage. Some problems additional reference material will solve, and some will remain a mystery.
- Come to the Bible with an eagerness to listen to Scripture as the Word of God and a willingness to hear and obey it. Trust the Holy Spirit to instruct you and to empower you through Scripture.

DISCIPLE
FAST TRACK

NEW TESTAMENT

"As Jesus continued on from there, he saw a man named Matthew sitting at a kiosk for collecting taxes. He said to him, 'Follow me,' and he got up and followed him."

—Matthew 9:9

1 Radical Discipleship

OUR HUMAN CONDITION

We are anxious. We conform to our culture, knowing all the while that it is sick and riddled with brokenness and confusion.

Jesus is a constant threat to our established ways. His lifestyle conflicts with our values. We hope he will go away; but when he keeps coming on, we reject, ridicule, and finally crucify him.

ASSIGNMENT

As you study and read Matthew, notice two different emphases: (1) the call to radical discipleship and (2) the mounting tension that led to Jesus' crucifixion. In the early portions of Matthew, look especially for value clashes, religious controversy, and political conflicts.

Then as you approach what is classically called the Passion (arrest, trial, the Crucifixion, and burial) and the Resurrection, read slowly and ponder.

Pray daily before study:

"Turn my heart to your laws,
    not to greedy gain.
Turn my eyes away from looking at
        worthless things.
    Make me live by your way.
Confirm your promise to your servant—
    the promise that is for all those who
        honor you" (Psalm 119:36-38).

Prayer concerns for the week:

Day 1 **Read Matthew 1–6** (birth narrative, radical discipleship).

Day 2 **Read Matthew 7–13** (the mission, secrets of the Kingdom).

Day 3 **Read Matthew 14–18** (life and leadership in the church, religious controversy).

Day 4 **Read Matthew 19–23** (entry into Jerusalem, being ready for judgment).

Day 5 **Read Matthew 24–28** (political conflicts, the Last Supper, the Resurrection, Great Commission).

Day 6 **Read "The Bible Teaching" and the "Marks of Discipleship" and answer the questions.**

Day 7 **Rest, pray, and attend class.**

THE BIBLE TEACHING

From the opening words of Matthew's Gospel, Matthew is making a statement: Jesus, the Son of David, has come to be the Savior for all humankind. His name was Jesus, a derivative of *Joshua*, meaning literally, "Yahweh is salvation."

Matthew arranged the genealogy into three groups of fourteen names each (Matthew 1:17). He omitted a few kings in order to achieve this neatness. But why three groups? Because Jewish history had three great stages: Abraham to David, David to exile in Babylon, and exile in Babylon to Jesus Christ. And women's names are included—most unusual in an ancient Jewish genealogy.

Matthew wanted his Jewish readers to understand that Jesus came first of all to his own people, the Jews. However, the wise men, who are thought to have been Gentiles "from the east," show that Jesus came to save Gentiles also.

Tension surrounding Jesus began with his birth. When the wise men from the east (Gentiles) asked, "Where is the newborn king of the Jews?" (Matthew 2:2), a political crisis arose. Herod the Great carried precisely that title, and he feared any other claimant to the throne. He was ruler of Judea at the time of Jesus' birth. He murdered his wife, his three sons, his mother-in-law, his brother-in-law, his uncle, and according to Matthew, all the children under two years old in Bethlehem to protect that title. He was one of the most important rulers in the Roman Empire, and his purpose was always to protect that status.

Jesus, by contrast, was born in a tiny village of Jewish peasant stock, a refugee in Egypt (like the Hebrew slaves), a carpenter in a poor section of the country. He had no wealth or political power and rejected the title of king (the common notion of Messiah was that of a political leader).

Matthew contrasts the Herods—powerful rulers and representatives of the Roman Empire—and Jesus, who filled the dual role of successor to King David and Son of God, the only true ruler of the Jews. The contrast and the conflict between the Herods and Jesus run through the Gospel from beginning to end.

The Call to Radical Discipleship

Jesus made an absolute demand. When he said, "Follow me," he meant leaving something or someone or some place behind. To obey meant to walk into the unknown unencumbered—ready to listen, to learn, to witness, to serve. The word *disciple* means "learner."

Simon and Andrew, James and John, left their fishing nets and relatives. Matthew, also called Levi, left his tax office. Jesus offered other persons radical discipleship, but they would not break loose from the things that held them. Jesus warned a scribe, a prospective disciple, that he would often be sleeping on the ground. We hear no more of the man (Matthew 8:19-20). Another wanted to wait until his elderly father died. "Follow me," said Jesus, and that man also faded (8:21-23). Still later a rich man considered discipleship. "Go, sell what you own . . . then . . . come follow me." But the man "went away saddened, because he had many possessions" (19:16-22). Even family members cannot stand in the way of discipleship (10:34-39). The Christian must have a single eye, seeking first God's kingdom and God's righteousness (6:33; read again 13:44-46).

The first word in Jesus' ministry was the word *repent* (4:17). From that time Jesus began to announce, "Repent, for the kingdom of heaven has come near" (NRSV).

Repent means not only to confess and be sorry for your sins but also, and more importantly, to turn around. *Repentance* means to change directions, have a new way of thinking and living, lead a new life.

The Sermon on the Mount (5–7) distills some of Jesus' most demanding statements:

- Speak only the truth.
- Do not lust even in your hearts.
- Root out rage from your emotions.
- Forgive without measure.
- Love your enemies.
- Pray privately.
- Wash your face when you fast so no one will know.
- Give without getting credit.
- Avoid being judgmental.
- Work for peace.

Jesus' concern for righteousness permeates the Sermon on the Mount. These Kingdom people will be a peculiar people. They will live lives of quiet gratitude, simply asking for daily bread, just like the Israelites receiving manna in the wilderness. If persecution comes, they should be grateful. Without doubt, these new disciples are expected to live a righteousness that "is greater than the righteousness of the legal experts and the Pharisees" (5:20).

What is the new righteousness? It is a life characterized by repentance, a life wrenched away from worldly living, now pointed in a fresh Kingdom direction.

Receiving forgiveness and new direction, disciples then extend forgiveness to others daily (as in the Lord's Prayer) and forever (as in seventy-seven times). So repentance speaks of new beginnings and of continually fresh commitments to the ways of God.

The Controversy

Jesus' preaching immediately became controversial. Jesus said he did not come to abolish the Law or the Prophets, but to fulfill them (Matthew 5:17-20). But look at how he interpreted the Law: "You have heard that it was said to those who lived long ago, *Don't commit murder*. . . . But I say to you that everyone who is angry with their brother or sister will be in danger of judgment" (5:21-22). No wonder the religious leaders began to ask, "Who does Jesus think he is to redefine the law of Moses? Where does he get his authority?"

Jesus' attack on superficiality was devastating, particularly in regard to religious pomp and hypocrisy.

As you read Matthew, notice Jesus' scathing denunciations of people who crave titles, places of honor, outward recognition (Matthew 6:1-7). Read again Matthew 23, the "woe" chapter, and recall Amos 4:1-5. We ought to tithe, Jesus said, but we dare not neglect weightier matters such as justice and mercy and faith (Matthew 23:23, NRSV).

Jesus challenges us economically too. We all worry about what clothes we'll wear, whether we will have enough food to eat. He said, "Gentiles [meaning those not of the people of God] long for all these things" (6:32). So we do. And to say God will clothe us and feed us if we "desire first and foremost God's kingdom and God's righteousness" (6:33) threatens our me-first, money-hungry society.

Tension With Religious Leaders

To understand the New Testament, we must know something about four influential religious groups of the period.

Pharisees. Laymen, not priests, forerunners of rabbis, teachers in local synagogues. Serious about interpreting and keeping the religious laws, including all the oral interpretations. Pharisees sat on "Moses' seat" in the synagogue with authority to interpret Scripture. They recognized Jesus as a teacher, hence the continued discussions. Theologically conservative, yet made room for mystery, freedom, resurrection. Great influence with the people. Some liberal, others conservative.

Essenes. Second largest group, scattered in all the towns, radically righteous. Thought everything in the Temple was wrong; believed the priests were illegitimate, the Temple corrupt. Rigid, legalistic, conservative. Celibate, no marriage, no children (except those adopted by the community). Ultra-scrupulous, prayed for Messiah, believed in "end times."

Sadducees. Priestly families, mostly living in Jerusalem and Jericho, descendants of Zadok who anointed Solomon. Aristocratic, wealthy, long-established families who assimilated much Greek and Roman culture. Believed God rewarded the good with health and wealth, punished the evil with sickness and poverty. No heaven or hell, no resurrection. Cooperated with Romans to preserve Temple worship and their own position. Controlled the Sanhedrin during Jesus' ministry. Their concern: Temple worship.

Zealots. Violently opposed the Roman occupation. Eager for revolt, praying for a Messiah-king to lead the uprising. Consisted of ex-slaves, superpatriots, and some bandits. Four beliefs: (a) served no one but God; (b) opposed slavery; (c) violently opposed Rome (don't pay taxes or cooperate; hide a sword in your bed; ready for Messiah); (d) preferred death, even by suicide, to slavery; willing to die for the cause.

Now let us see why Jesus came into conflict with these religious groups. Abraham and the other ancestors were blessed in order to be a blessing (Genesis 12:2-3). Israel is to be a light to the nations (Isaiah 42:6). Instead, however, close fellowship evolved into smugness, Sabbath observance became a set of rules, and food laws made fellowship with others impossible. God, Creator of the universe, it was thought, had taken up residence in the Temple in Jerusalem. Greek culture was shunned; Roman soldiers were despised.

When Jesus said of the Roman centurion, "I say to you with all seriousness that even in Israel I haven't found faith like this" (Matthew 8:10), his statement offended the Zealots. When he ate with ceremonially unclean people at Matthew's dinner, his action offended the Pharisees in particular, because they were meticulous in keeping food laws and avoiding sinners as a form of righteousness (9:10-13). Jesus, like Hosea and Amos, argued that steadfast love took precedence over ceremony (see Hosea 6:6; Amos 5:21-24). But Jesus went further than the prophets: He came precisely to bring sinners, outcasts, and alienated people into fellowship.

Jesus' inclusiveness offended. Jewish men of the times offered a daily prayer thanking God that they had not been born a slave, a Gentile, or a woman. Matthew stresses Jesus' attention to the poor, the marginalized, the untouchable, and the foreigner.

The Mission

Disciples are not just "to be." They are called "to do." The community of faith is thrust into mission. A leper cried out and was healed (Matthew 8:2-4). A Roman officer, a centurion in charge of one hundred soldiers, asked help for a paralyzed servant. Amazed at the faith of the Gentile soldier, Jesus remarked, "There are many who will come from east and west and sit down to eat with Abraham and Isaac and Jacob in the kingdom of heaven" (8:5-13). The servant was healed.

Next Jesus did what only God can do—forgive sins. The paralytic was healed. Then, Jesus called Matthew the tax collector to be a disciple. At Matthew's dinner party, amid criticism for eating with the tax collectors who were ceremonially unclean and were hated because they collected Roman taxes, Jesus was still claiming people: "I didn't come to call righteous people, but sinners" (9:13).

Now watch: The work of the Kingdom is designed to explode in magnitude. Jesus said to the disciples, "The size of the harvest is bigger than you can imagine, but there are few workers. Therefore, plead with the Lord of the harvest to send out workers for his harvest" (9:37-38). Jesus actually expected the disciples to do the same things he had been doing! At first they are to go only to the Jews. Later they will go to the whole world. "As you go, make this announcement: 'The kingdom of heaven has come near.' Heal the sick, raise the dead, cleanse those with skin diseases, and throw out demons" (10:7-8).

Rabbis used the term *yoke* in reference to the Law. What did Jesus mean by "Put on my yoke, and learn from me. I'm gentle and humble. And you will find rest for yourselves" (11:29)?

If Jesus calls us to radical discipleship, in what sense is his yoke easy and his burden light (11:30)?

A Different Messiah

Jesus wanted his disciples to be more concerned about moral law than ceremonial law. Some Jewish teachers, building on oral tradition, were "majoring in minors." Some rabbis taught that people should wash their hands ritualistically seven times before and after a meal. Jesus focused on spiritual matters: "Out of the heart come evil thoughts, murders, adultery, sexual sins, thefts, false testimonies, and insults" (Matthew 15:19).

Tension mounted when Jesus confronted the disciples in Caesarea Philippi, asking, "Who do you say that I am?" (Matthew 16:15). He was doing two things: establishing their faith in him as Messiah and, equally important, clarifying what kind of Messiah he was to be. "Jesus began to show his disciples that he had to go to Jerusalem and suffer many things from the elders, chief priests, and legal experts, and that he had to be killed and raised on the third day" (16:21). The people thought Messiah would come in power, a conquering hero on a white horse.

Jesus moved the disciples to an even deeper level. The Messiah is going to suffer. The Christian community will suffer as well. But look at what happened. When Jesus said that he must go to Jerusalem to suffer, Peter protested. Jesus rebuked him severely (Matthew 16:22-23). Why? Because Jesus was walking the way of the cross. We will walk it also. The cross of Jesus will be the standard for the Christian community. We will be saved by that cross. We will live by that cross.

Watching and Waiting

The Christian community, with the leadership of the Anointed One, is both experiencing a foretaste of the Kingdom and awaiting the Kingdom's complete fulfillment.

So, as we wait and watch, we are to be faithful to our spouses (Matthew 19:3-9) or single for Kingdom work (19:10-12), gentle and loving with children (19:13-15), and unconcerned about getting rich (19:23-30). All will get the same salvation whether early in life or at the eleventh hour, for salvation is not earned. It is given us out of the grace of God (20:1-16). Leaders in the church are those who serve most humbly and most faithfully (20:20-28).

Jesus carefully orchestrated the entry into Jerusalem. On one hand, the Anointed One must bring the Kingdom encounter to Jerusalem. On the other hand, people must, at least in retrospect, understand what kind of Messiah he is. He must try to present Messiah not as a political king like David but as God's compassionate and holy, yet vulnerable, Son-Messenger.

Gathering Storm

The religious leaders were afraid of Jesus, because if Jesus stirred up trouble, the Romans would come down hard on them. An insurrection could destroy everyone, especially the Temple.

When the Pharisees asked Jesus to quiet the crowd on Palm Sunday (Luke 19:39-40), they were afraid the Roman soldiers would see them as an unruly mob disturbing the peace and would kill hundreds.

Who killed Jesus? No one wanted to take the blame. The Sanhedrin, though offended by Jesus' teachings, though certain of his blasphemy, wanted him executed by Rome. So they charged him not with breaking the Jewish law but with sedition. Pilate tried to pass the buck to Herod Antipas, who had killed John the Baptist. But Herod had to go back to Galilee, where Jesus was popular. Pilate flogged Jesus, which meant almost certain death through loss of blood, infection, or tetanus. No wonder Jesus could not carry his cross.

When Sanhedrin leaders demanded Jesus' death as an enemy of Rome, Pilate did the deed yet put the blame on the religious leaders once again. The title *King of the Jews* meant another insurrectionist had been stamped out.

Who killed Jesus? Every hand lifted in anger, every lie, every act of self-interest. You and I and all the sinners of the world drove the nails.

MARKS OF DISCIPLESHIP

Can you see how often the church makes discipleship seem too easy? "Accept Jesus Christ as your Lord and Savior" is so true but often superficial, lacking the radical demands, the total commitment of discipleship: Give up everything and follow Jesus.

Describe where you are in your discipleship. Have you responded to Christ's call, "Follow me"? Is anything or anyone holding you back?

NOTES

Mark of Discipleship
Disciples accept Christ's call to radical discipleship, abandoning sham and pretense, becoming vulnerable, and entering the ministry of making disciples.

How is radical discipleship the answer to our need to conform to culture and the status quo?

In what areas of your life does Jesus continue to threaten your values, your lifestyle?

As a participant in the Kingdom community, what tension, if any, are you encountering in society? in the economic or political system? with your neighbors and friends? in your church?

IF YOU WANT TO KNOW MORE

The Sermon on the Mount (Matthew 5–7) contains some of the highest ethical insights ever proclaimed. Study it carefully. The

Beatitudes (5:3-12) are the "essence of the essence." Paraphrase the eight Beatitudes in your own words.

In a Bible dictionary, look up the following people who were involved in the Crucifixion and jot down a descriptive note or two about each one: Judas Iscariot, Caiaphas, Pilate, Barabbas, Simon of Cyrene, Mary Magdalene, Joseph of Arimathea, Herod Antipas (see Luke 23:6-12).

SPECIAL ASSIGNMENT

Because the commands are clear in Matthew 25, make one visit during the week to one of the following places or persons: a drug rehabilitation center, a rescue mission, a hospital, a person with cancer, a nursing home, a jail or penitentiary, a person who is homebound, a person with a handicapping condition, a shelter for the homeless, a teenager who does not go to church, a person on social welfare, a person of another culture. If appropriate, take a small gift (toothpaste to jail, cookies to homebound persons, reading material, flowers). Don't do all the talking; be there to listen. Especially try to go into a situation where you have never been before. Be ready to tell the group members next week about your experience and what you learned about yourself.

"Now is the time! Here comes God's kingdom! Change your hearts and lives, and trust this good news!"

—Mark 1:15

2 The Hidden Messiah

OUR HUMAN CONDITION

Like the disciples, we do not understand who Jesus is. Sometimes we half understand, or misunderstand, or refuse to understand. We especially close our eyes and ears to his call for *self-denial* and *suffering.* This "good news" sounds like bad news to us.

ASSIGNMENT

When you read Mark's Gospel, notice the urgency, the sense of intensity and movement. Observe Mark's emphasis on Jesus' actions. Watch for the word *immediately*.

Pray daily before study:

"God, your way is holiness!
   Who is as great a god as you, God?
You are the God who works wonders;
   you have demonstrated your strength
     among all peoples" (Psalm 77:13-14).

Prayer concerns for the week:

GOOD NEWS

Day 1 Read Mark 1–4 (call of the Twelve, parables of the Kingdom).

Day 2 Read Mark 5–8 (preaching and healing).

Day 3 Read Mark 9–11 (Transfiguration, entry into Jerusalem).

Day 4 Read Mark 12–14 (Great Commission, the Last Supper, the arrest).

Day 5 Read Mark 15–16 (the Crucifixion, the Resurrection).

Day 6 Read "The Bible Teaching" and the "Marks of Discipleship."

Day 7 Rest, pray, and attend class.

DISCIPLE FAST TRACK

THE BIBLE TEACHING

As you read Mark's Gospel, you may think, "Haven't I read this before?" You have, in Matthew. Both Matthew and Luke may have had the Gospel of Mark in front of them as they wrote. Many scholars think Mark was the first Gospel written. Matthew, Mark, and Luke are called the Synoptic Gospels. *Synoptic* means "seen together." They have much common material.

Mark has a special thrust. The Son of God proclaims the Kingdom and demands repentance—now! Mark is the urgent evangelist. His Gospel is filled with action. The pace is rapid. The word *immediately* appears twenty-seven times. Mark also shows that people did not understand until after the Crucifixion and Resurrection that Jesus was a "hidden Messiah."

Mark does not record the birth narratives, the Sermon on the Mount, or many of the parables. Instead he starts with Jesus' baptism and ends with the Resurrection, giving a short, powerful account of the ministry of Jesus.

The opening verse sets the stage: "The beginning of the good news about Jesus Christ, God's Son" (Mark 1:1). Mark will write about the good news of Jesus the promised Messiah, strong Son of God, sent to save. He will show how the disciples were slow to understand, especially when the idea of suffering entered the picture.

In our study of Mark we will emphasize the power of Jesus Christ, the mystery of who he was and what his ministry was to be before the Crucifixion and Resurrection events, and the good news we now can receive.

The ministry begins with the baptism of Jesus by his relative John. The Holy Spirit came upon Jesus, and his powerful ministry was ready to begin.

Jesus went into the wilderness, alone with the desolation, the animals, Satan (meaning "adversary"), and the angels. He stayed for forty days, symbolic of the Israelites' forty years in the Sinai, in conflict with Satan, hammering out the nature of his ministry on the anvil of prayer and fasting.

Jesus emerged from the wilderness preaching his first, and essential, sermon: "Now is the time! Here comes God's kingdom! Change your hearts and lives, and trust this good news!" (Mark 1:15).

The people believed that someday God's kingdom would come when nations would "beat their swords into iron plows" (Isaiah 2:4), when those who were blind would see and those who were hungry would not be turned away (Psalm 146). What happened? Jesus brought signs of the Kingdom. He healed a man who was blind, fed the multitude. The prophecies were being fulfilled!

The Jews were expecting God to act in such a way that God's rule would be acclaimed by Israel and the world. Instead, a carpenter came out of Nazareth, announcing, "Here comes God's kingdom! Change your hearts and lives" (Mark 1:15). Men and women were called to participate in the Kingdom—to change or to be changed radically into citizens of a new society, a new reign, a new way of living.

Jesus announced the Kingdom; even more, he ushered in the Kingdom. But his people were praying for a political Messiah; the Romans feared social unrest and political revolt. Jesus continually tried to interpret his kingdom, but people could not understand.

When Jesus preached or taught or healed, he announced the reign of God. When he prayed, broke bread, took a child in his arms, touched a leper, he activated the rule of God. God's power and kingdom were present in the words and acts of Jesus. That Jesus had power there was no doubt. But Mark emphasizes the mysterious power that would not be understood until after the Resurrection. Even the signs of the Kingdom were misinterpreted as signs of a hoped-for political Messiah.

Power Over Unclean Spirits

The most dramatic story of our Lord's power over unclean spirits is Mark 5:1-20. The man hurt himself, screamed, lived among the tombs. He said his name was Legion, "because we are many" (5:9). What do you think was the matter with him?

Jesus drove an unclean spirit out of the man. The unclean spirit understood that it was confronting the power of God, but the people did not understand.

Power Over Disease and Physical Problems

Jesus "healed many who were sick with all kinds of diseases" (Mark 1:34). In Mark 1:40-42, Jesus healed a man who was sick with a skin disease. The healings were signs of the Kingdom, because where God's rule is acknowledged, disease is brought under God's power and control.

But some physical problems are caused by accident, not disease. Others are present from birth. Jesus did not restrict his healing to the sick. The man who was deaf (7:32-35) was not sick, had not sinned, was not ceremonially unclean. He could not hear and did not speak clearly. Jesus made him whole.

The Son of God was and is working to restore God's original harmonious creation. In Romans 8:21-22, Paul declared that "creation itself will be set free from slavery to decay. . . . The whole creation is groaning together and suffering labor pains up until now."

Power Over Sin

Jesus dismissed the popular notion that all illness or infirmity was caused by sin (John 9:1-3). But in Mark 2:1-12, the man's problem was sin and his need was forgiveness. His friends lowered their helpless companion through an opening in the roof.

What do you believe about whether sin and guilt can cause physical or emotional illness?

In your own experience, have you observed Jesus' power to forgive sins? Describe specific examples.

Mark's Gospel wants us to know that forgiveness and God's kingdom go together and that Jesus has the power to forgive sins.

Power Over Sabbath

Recall that the Creation story in Genesis 1:1–2:3 was given to us to teach us to trust God and rest one day in seven. A saying of the Jews was, "We keep the Sabbath; God keeps us." In Jesus' day nothing was more precious, yet nothing had become more complicated with protective laws and teachings than Sabbath. The technical word for these laws and teachings meant "hedge" or "fence." Build a hedge around the Sabbath to be sure it would not be violated. The day of rest (Friday sundown until Saturday sundown) had become a legal confusion. Sabbath keeping was difficult for some, tedious for others.

The issue is drawn sharply in Mark 3:1-6. Jewish law permitted medical attention on the Sabbath to save a person's life. A paralyzed hand could wait. Jesus deliberately asked the Pharisees if he could "do good" on the Sabbath but got no answer. So Jesus' view was, "The Sabbath was created for humans; humans weren't created for the Sabbath. This is why the Human One is Lord even over the Sabbath" (2:27-28). It is all right to do good, to heal, to extend mercy. Sabbath is to restore, not to bind up.

The early Christians rested on Sabbath, the seventh day, and also worshiped on Resurrection Day, the first day of the week. By early second century A.D., the first day of the week, Sunday, had become Sabbath to them. Sunday became "the Lord's day" for most Gentile Christians, although to this day there are some who observe the seventh day. Jewish Christians in Judea kept Sabbath for a long time.

How are you being "re-created" on Sunday?

Some say that today we abuse the freedom we feel toward our use of our Sabbath. What do you think?

Power Over Nature

There is disharmony. Mark records several times when Jesus exercised power over nature. He stilled the storm (Mark 4:35-41). He walked on the water (6:45-52).

Jesus' word was the word of power: "Be encouraged! . . . Don't be afraid" (6:50). Mark declares that the disciples did not understand with whom they were dealing. They were awestruck and confused.

Feeding the five thousand (6:30-44) was also an evidence of power over nature. What a Kingdom sign!

How do you feel when you break bread in the fellowship of the church?

How do you feel when you share food with someone who is really hungry (or has that ever happened)?

Power Over Death

The account of Jesus' raising Jairus's daughter from the dead (Mark 5:22-24, 35-43) has two problems. First, did Jesus have power to raise the dead? Second, was Jairus's daughter really dead? Mark gives us the story the way he received it. The early church had no doubt that Jesus had that power.

More important for Mark was Jesus' teaching about resurrection. He clearly told the Sadducees that their disbelief in resurrection was wrong (12:18-27).

Most important, Mark was leading up to our Lord's resurrection. When Jesus was raised from the dead, it made the matter of Jairus's daughter a moot point. Whether she was in a coma or whether Jesus referred to death as "sleeping" became insignificant. Her raising was another sign of the Kingdom.

What do you think about Jesus' power over death?

DISCIPLE FAST TRACK

The Hidden Messiah

NOTES

Did you wonder, as you read Mark, why Jesus kept telling people to be quiet, not to tell others? For example, when unclean spirits cried out, " 'You are God's Son!' . . . he strictly ordered them not to reveal who he was" (Mark 3:11-12). After raising the twelve-year-old daughter of Jairus, "he gave them strict orders that no one should know what had happened" (5:43). He went to the region of Tyre and "didn't want anyone to know that he had entered a house, but he couldn't hide" (7:24). When Peter said, "You are the Christ," Jesus "ordered them not to tell anyone about him" (8:29-30). When Peter, James, and John came down the mountain after the Transfiguration, Jesus "ordered them not to tell anyone what they had seen until after the Human One had risen from the dead" (9:9).

Why the mystery? Why the secrecy? With all the spiritual power being exhibited, why the request to keep it quiet?

Mark even suggests that Jesus used parables so people would not understand. At least Mark says that Jesus "spoke to them only in parables, then explained everything to his disciples when he was alone with them" (4:34).

Didn't Jesus want people to know? Yes, but to know what? That is the point. They must have a right understanding of Messiah. Jesus was not using reverse psychology, as some have suggested, telling people to be quiet, knowing that would make them even more talkative.

Jesus knew the people were not understanding who he was. They wanted his power to be Davidic; Jesus knew his power would be vulnerable love. They would wave palm branches and try to make him king; he would ride humbly on a donkey. They would see the healings as magic or miracle; he wanted the healings to call people to repentance and faith. Jesus was not running a sideshow or building momentum for a power play. He was preparing to offer himself as a sacrifice for the sins of the whole world.

He tried to explain to the disciples, but even they could not understand the nature of his relationship to God, the character of the Kingdom, the power of his suffering servant role until he was crucified and raised from the dead.

Jesus offered the world his power. Before Mark 14:36, he was in control. After the garden, he placed himself in the hands of others.

Tradition taught that Messiah would come to the Mount of Olives and then in power enter Jerusalem. Jesus transformed the meaning of that tradition. *Gethsemane*, on the Mount of Olives, means "oil press." Jesus, in prayer, was "pressed out" into sacramental oil for blessing the people.

22

Jesus did what love does: He placed himself in the hands of others. So when Judas kissed him, when Peter denied him, when men spat upon him, Messiah was being reinterpreted. When the soldiers stripped him naked for crucifixion, as was the custom, they took his garments, one each—his head turban, his belt, his sandals, and his outer robe—and gambled for the inner tunic. It was the symbol, like the body on the cross, of total helplessness, total vulnerability, love laid open.

Thus, when Jesus said, "It is completed" (John 19:30), he meant he had given the world the active power of God's love and the passive helplessness of God's love. He gave it all.

MARKS OF DISCIPLESHIP

The disciple understands Messiah as suffering servant and the Kingdom as a rule of vulnerable love. How, then, would you describe the ministry of the disciple of this Messiah, in this Kingdom?

Mark of Discipleship
Disciples understand their ministry as a call to self-denial and suffering.

A parishioner said to her pastor, "I know Jesus as my Savior. I do not know him as my Lord." What do you think she meant?

Most people see power in huge business enterprises, great political organizations, or mighty military machines. Christ's power seems hidden, weak, vulnerable. Yet Christians see a mighty spiritual power in Jesus. Have you ever experienced the power of Jesus Christ? When and how?

IF YOU WANT TO KNOW MORE

Levi was a tax collector (Mark 2:14-17). So was Zacchaeus (Luke 19:2). What was a tax collector? How were they perceived and treated? Look up *tax collectors* or *publicans* in a Bible dictionary.

Check the footnotes in your study Bible at the end of Mark for a discussion of the various endings of that Gospel.

"The Spirit of the Lord is upon me, because the Lord has anointed me. He has sent me to preach good news to the poor, to proclaim release to the prisoners and recovery of sight to the blind, to liberate the oppressed, and to proclaim the year of the Lord's favor."
—Luke 4:18-19

3 God Seeks the Least, the Last, and the Lost

OUR HUMAN CONDITION

I don't really like the poor. They're not always clean. I stay away from sick people. They smell bad. I don't understand people whose customs, culture, and ways of thinking are different from mine. They make me feel uncomfortable. I don't want to go to church with them or socialize with them. People with disabilities also make me feel awkward. Actually, I enjoy being with people who are just like me.

ASSIGNMENT

Although we want to read all of Luke this week, we want to move quickly through material Luke has in common with Matthew and Mark and focus on material that is unique to Luke's Gospel.

Pray daily before study:

"I'm poor and needy.
    Hurry to me, God!
You are my helper and my deliverer.
    Oh, LORD, don't delay!" (Psalm 70:5).

Prayer concerns for the week:

Day 1 **Read Luke 1–2; 4:1-13** (Jesus' birth and childhood, temptation).

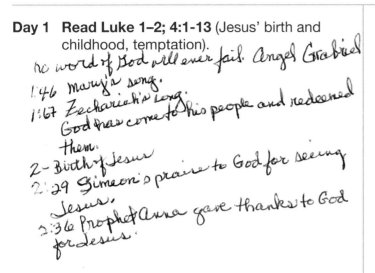

no word of God will ever fail. Angel Grabiel
1:46 Mary's song.
1:67 Zechariah's song.
God has come to his people and redeemed them.
2 - Birth of Jesus
2:29 Simeon's praise to God for seeing Jesus.
2:36 Prophet Anna gave thanks to God for Jesus.

Luke was a physian

Day 2 **Read Luke 4:14–9:50** (Jesus' announcement of his mission, healing miracles, dispute about greatness).

Day 3 **Read Luke 9:51–12:59** (mission of the seventy, parables of watchfulness and faithfulness).

Day 4 **Read Luke 13–15** (parables of the lost); **16:1–19:27** (parables of stewardship and prayer, Zacchaeus).

Day 5 **Read Luke 19:28–24:53** (entry into Jerusalem, Passion, Resurrection, walk to Emmaus).

Day 6 **Read "The Bible Teaching" and the "Marks of Discipleship" and answer the questions.**

Day 7 **Rest, pray, and attend class.**

THE BIBLE TEACHING

The Gospel of Luke is the first volume of the two-volume work Luke-Acts. The first verses of Luke and of Acts help us understand why and how each book was written. Read again Luke 1:1-4. Who was Theophilus? Apparently he was a socially prominent Gentile Christian. The name means "lover of God." Look to see how the second volume (Acts) begins.

The Birth of Jesus

Uniquely in Luke we read about the birth of John the Baptist, Jesus' relative, who became the forerunner:

> "A voice crying out in the wilderness:
>   'Prepare the way for the Lord'"
>   (Luke 3:4; see Isaiah 40:3).

The words of the angel Gabriel to Mary (Luke 1:28, KJV) are the basis for the prayer used widely in the Roman Catholic Church, "Hail, Mary, full of grace." Martin Luther translated this prayer simply, "liebe Maria," dear Mary, "the Lord is with you" (1:28).

In Mary's song, the powerful Magnificat (1:46-55), Mary set the tone for Luke's Gospel—the mighty action of God on behalf of the poor.

Luke records the visit of the shepherds. Keeping watch over sheep at night was a miserable job—a job for men who were old or crippled, or boys too poor or too young for other work. They were the "least" who heard the angels and knelt first at the manger (2:8-20).

Mary and Joseph kept the Jewish law and tradition by having Jesus circumcised on the eighth day (2:21). (Remember Abraham and the covenant people; Genesis 17:9-14.) The rite of purification for Mary came forty days after Jesus' birth. Joseph and Mary offered a poor woman's sacrifice, two turtledoves instead of a lamb (Luke 2:22-24; see Leviticus 12). The mother of the Lamb of God could not afford a lamb to sacrifice.

When Simeon took Jesus in his arms (Luke 2:25-35), he offered a poem of faith, now called the *Nunc Dimittis* (from the opening words of the prayer in Latin, translated as "Now, master, let your servant go in peace"). This prayer (2:29-32) is used regularly in many Roman Catholic and Protestant services of worship and daily in evening prayers.

Notice that Simeon also established Luke's theme of the universality of Christ's mission:

> "It's a light for revelation to the Gentiles
>   and a glory for your people Israel" (2:32).

Luke again emphasizes the universality of Jesus' ministry in his genealogy (3:23-38), which traces Jesus' ancestors back to Adam rather than only to Abraham.

The devotion of Joseph and Mary to the law and tradition is evident not only in their observance of the rites of circumcision and purification but also in their annual Passover trip to Jerusalem (2:41). Going to Jerusalem every year was expensive for poor people because of oppressive taxes, especially Roman "travel" taxes.

Temptation

As we have seen in Matthew and Mark, Jesus fasted and prayed for forty days in the wilderness. Luke gives more details on the temptation than does Mark. It was a soul-shattering test.

Break your fast. Turn stones to bread (Luke 4:1-4). Daily manna is necessary, but Jesus remembered Torah and rebuked the devil: "People don't live on bread alone. No, they live based on whatever the LORD says" (Deuteronomy 8:3; see Luke 4:4). Jesus' ministry was for a deep hunger, a hunger of the soul for God.

"Therefore, if you will worship me, it [authority over the kingdoms of the world] will all be yours," said the devil (4:6-7). Political reform might help the poor. But the price? Reenact Eve and Adam in the garden. Disobey as King Saul did. Fall into the passion of David. Rebel in arrogance as Solomon did. Then you can rule mighty empires. But Jesus said no: "It's written, *You will worship the Lord your God and serve only him*" (Luke 4:8; see Deuteronomy 6:13).

Jesus must have remembered that nonpolitical vow later when he mounted a donkey for his humble entry into Jerusalem and when he said to Pilate, "My kingdom doesn't originate from this world" (John 18:36). The Jews wanted a political leader; Jesus gave the world a Savior.

Next the devil himself quoted Scripture. Do a mighty sign! Jump off the Temple! Draw a crowd! For as the psalmist said, "*He will command his angels concerning you*" (Luke 4:10; see Psalm 91:11). What an opportunity to preach the gospel, suggested the devil. Maybe the common people would believe.

No. Jesus again reached into Torah: "*Don't test the Lord your God*" (Luke 4:12; see Deuteronomy 6:16). Then the Bible says that the devil "departed from him until the next opportunity" (Luke 4:13).

Thinking now of the life of Jesus, when do you suppose other "opportunities" of testing came to him?

In the garden.

Christians have always been grateful to know about the terrible, agonizing temptation of Jesus. His experience helps us when we are struggling. The writer of Hebrews put it dramatically: "Because we don't have a high priest who can't sympathize with our weaknesses but instead one who was tempted in every way that we are, except without sin. Finally, let's draw near to the throne of favor with confidence so that we can receive mercy and find grace when we need help" (Hebrews 4:15-16).

At Home in Nazareth

The Judaism of Jesus' day took two forms: worship through sacrifices in the Temple and, for study of Scriptures in Jewish communities all over the world, the synagogue.

Jesus went to his hometown synagogue "as he normally did" (Luke 4:16). He found and read the familiar passage from Isaiah 61. Notice the focus on those who are poor, blind, oppressed. No problem—until Jesus laid claim to the role of the Anointed One— that is, the Messiah—and announced the time. To make the point that, though the Messiah would be rejected by his own people, his ministry would extend to the whole world (Luke 4:24-27), Jesus reminded the people of the Phoenician widow who received Elijah and of the Syrian general, Naaman, cured of leprosy by Elisha. The people were furious and tried to kill him (4:28-30). So began his ministry.

Samaritans

You will remember that the Samaritans were descendants of Israelites who across the centuries had intermarried with their Gentile neighbors. They had lived in what had been the Northern Kingdom, ravaged by invading armies and often cut off from Jerusalem. A North-South prejudice developed, because for centuries now the Samaritans had worshiped at Mount Gerizim near the old Canaanite city of Shechem; the Southerners—the Judeans and their purer Jewish descendants—had worshiped in Jerusalem.

At the time of Jesus the bitterness was intense. Jews traveling from the north would normally cross over the Jordan to the east so they would not have to walk through Samaria. The Samaritans used only the first five books of the Bible, the Torah, because they believed only those books had been given directly by God. They had a distinctive celebration of Passover, strictly following the procedure in Exodus 12 for sacrificing the Passover lamb. The Jews and the Samaritans despised each other.

Jesus, when he left Galilee, "determined to go to Jerusalem" and went directly through Samaria. But the Samaritan people would not receive him because he was on his way to Jerusalem. The disciples wanted to bring fire from heaven to burn them up. But Jesus rebuked the disciples (Luke 9:51-56).

When Jesus answered the lawyer's question, "Who is my neighbor?" (10:29), he told a story of a man who was attacked by robbers on the road between Jerusalem and Jericho. Was the man dead? If so, a Jew who touched him would become ceremonially unclean. Did the priest help him? Did the Levite? Who helped? A Samaritan—a hated half-breed, a foreigner (10:29-37). Jesus deliberately chose a Samaritan to be the hero of his story.

Later Jesus healed ten lepers who stood beside the road in quarantine calling "unclean, unclean." Only one of them stopped to say thanks, and "he was a Samaritan" (17:16). When people experience pain, tragedy, and terrible disease, social barriers break down, as they had for the ten lepers. Later we will see that the blood of Jesus also breaks down these barriers.

Women

In all the Gospels, Jesus reached out to women with tenderness and compassion. He treated women with dignity. Luke's Gospel especially emphasizes Jesus' attitudes toward women. The birth narratives show Elizabeth, Mary, and Anna with great personal strength and spiritual maturity.

In the town of Nain, Jesus raised from the dead the only son of a widow. Luke records, "[He] had compassion for her and said, 'Don't cry'" (Luke 7:13). Another woman, whose sins were "many" but who wept at Jesus' feet, not only received forgiveness but became an example for the Pharisees of the deep meaning of love (7:36-50).

Apparently several women traveled with Jesus and the disciples, providing money and food and encouragement: Mary Magdalene, "from whom seven demons had been thrown out"; Joanna, the wife of Chuza, Herod's steward (a rather prominent woman); Susanna; and many others, "who provided for them out of their resources" (8:1-3).

Perhaps Mary, the sister of Martha, best revealed what was happening in this social revolution that now included women. Normally, men talked about the Law and the Prophets. Remember Job said he used to sit at the gate of the city and talk with the men about deep matters (Job 29:7-12). The idealized woman in Proverbs 31, while she worked with her household, took pride that

> "Her husband is known in the city gates,
>   when he sits with the elders of the land"
> > (Proverbs 31:23).

But Mary "sat at the Lord's feet and listened to his message" (Luke 10:39). In response to Martha's criticism, Jesus replied, "Mary has chosen the better part. It won't be taken away from her" (10:42).

How did Jesus redefine a woman's role?

tenderness, compassion, strength, spiritual maturity, provider, love

The Lost

The parables of the lost are found in Luke 15: the lost sheep, the lost coin, and the lost son or lost sons. (Some call this the parable

NOTES

of the waiting father.) No one was more "lost" in the eyes of the Jews than the tax collectors and publicans who contracted with the Romans to collect taxes. They were seen as aiding Roman domination and were ostracized.

Look through Luke's Gospel and see when tax collectors were especially included in Jesus' ministry. Do not overlook Zacchaeus or Levi or the parable of the Pharisee and the tax collector. List the tax collector episodes with your comments.

MARKS OF DISCIPLESHIP

We can look at the least, the last, and the lost in two ways. One way is to think of people who fall into those categories. Who are the poor today?

Who are the social outcasts?

What are you or your church doing to include them in the grace and fellowship of your community of faith?

Mark of Discipleship
Disciples throw their weight with God's mission to the least, the last, the lost.

What kind of criticism are you likely to receive for including them?

The other way to look at the least, the last, and the lost is to include ourselves in that group. Some of us are women. Most of us are Gentiles. Some of us are poor. All of us have been sick. A few have abused alcohol or drugs. Some of us have been publicly shamed. Some have been in jail. For some, divorce or death of a spouse or being single is a social stigma. Paul wrote to the Corinthians (and to us), "By ordinary human standards, not many were wise, not many were powerful, not many were from the upper class. But God chose what the world considers foolish to shame the wise. God chose what the world considers weak to shame the strong. And God chose what the world considers low-class— what is considered to be nothing—to reduce what is considered to be something to nothing. So no human being can brag in God's presence" (1 Corinthians 1:26-29).

In your experience, have you ever felt outcast, ashamed, cut off, or "unclean"? If so, what was it like? What helped you overcome that feeling?

Deep down, disciples know that their wealth, power, and prestige will not save them. Deep down, disciples know they are desperately in need of Jesus Christ's grace. Deep down, disciples understand that God has a special concern to include the outcast, the marginalized, the widow, the orphan, the dispossessed, and the exploited. Disciples throw their weight with God's mission to the least, the last, and the lost.

IF YOU WANT TO KNOW MORE

If you have time, compare the trial, Crucifixion, and Resurrection accounts in the four Gospels. Make notes on the uniqueness of each account.

"I came so that they could have life—indeed, so that they could live life to the fullest." —John 10:10

4 Lifegiver

OUR HUMAN CONDITION

Most of the time life seems meaningless. What is the point of living? I try to get close to others, but often I feel cut off. How can I live a happy, productive life, at peace with myself and others? I want more than religion or religious ceremony. I want to experience God as a living presence in my life. I want to live with spiritual power.

ASSIGNMENT

In the first half of John's Gospel, we study life, abundant and eternal. The theme of the second part will be the Holy Spirit promised by Jesus Christ. Look for these symbols: bread, water, light, life, shepherd, gate. Also look for vivid contrasts: light and darkness, truth and lies, life and death, love and hate.

Nowhere in the Gospels are the demands of discipleship stated more forcefully than in the Gospel of John. Watch for the promises of the presence and power of the Holy Spirit for meeting those demands.

Pray daily before study:

"How precious, O God, is your
     constant love!
  We find protection under the shadow
     of your wings.
We feast on the abundant food you
     provide;
  you let us drink from the river of your
     goodness.
You are the source of all life,
  and because of your light we see
     the light" (Psalm 36:7-9, GNT).

Prayer concerns for the week:

Day 1 **Read John 1–5** (Word become flesh, miracle at Cana, born from above, woman of Samaria, healing the sick).

Day 2 **Read John 6–9** (bread of life, living water, light of the world, teaching in the Temple, blind man healed).

Day 3 **Read John 10–13** (good shepherd, Lazarus, entry into Jerusalem, "believe in the light").

Day 4 **Read John 14–17** (coming of the Companion, true vine, Spirit of truth, Jesus' prayer for his disciples).

Day 5 **Read John 18–21** (arrest and trials, Crucifixion, Resurrection, appearance to the disciples and by the sea, instruction to Peter).

Day 6 **Read "The Bible Teaching" and the "Marks of Discipleship" and answer the questions.**

Day 7 **Rest, pray, and attend class.**

DISCIPLE FAST TRACK

THE BIBLE TEACHING

The Gospel writers were not biographers. Rather, they were evangelists, especially John, trying to help their readers know and follow the Son of God.

Think now of the issue of life and death.

So when the Lifegiver comes, he brings life into the here and now, into the "inside" of a person where meaninglessness resides. Life is not a gift after death; life is a gift to the believer *now*.

As Martha met Jesus after her brother Lazarus's death and confessed, "I believe that you are the Messiah, the Son of God, the one coming into the world" (11:27), life was born within her. Fear was changed to trust, loneliness to companionship, pretense to openness. What God had wanted for Adam and Eve was happening in Martha.

Notice that the raising of Lazarus was a dramatic confrontation. Jesus used the event to teach the disciples that he was Lord of death. But others were offended. The Pharisees were upset because people were flocking to listen to Jesus and to see Lazarus. So the chief priests planned to put Lazarus to death also, because on his account many Jews were believing in Jesus (12:9-11, 17-19).

Now we have a clearer view of Nicodemus and his needs. He was probably a better Jew than most of us are Christians. He kept the Law. But he was empty inside. He was hungry, not for religion but for God. Jesus said he needed to be born into life, "born from above," "born anew" (3:3).

The Woman at the Well

If you go to Jacob's well today, you can still drink water from it. The well is 105 feet deep, located near the site of ancient Shechem. Shechem, sometimes translated "Sychar," was a religious and political center. Joshua renewed the Sinai covenant with the leaders of the tribes of Israel at Shechem. Long before that, and nearly two thousand years before Jesus, Abraham, Isaac, and Jacob grazed their flocks there. Jacob bought a field near Shechem, dug a well, and gave it to his son Joseph. Later Joseph's bones were buried at Shechem (Joshua 24:32). Shechem was in the heart of what was later called Samaria.

As we have learned, Jews would not speak to Samaritans. They would walk across the road to avoid social contact. If a Samaritan's shadow fell across the path of a law-abiding Jew, the Jew would go to the Temple for cleansing. When Jews spoke the word *Samaritan*, they would utter a curse and spit on the ground. Samaritans sometimes would follow Jews, put bits of straw in their tracks, and set fire to the straw. Good riddance, they would think.

Jesus sat down, in hostile territory, looking to one side at Mount Gerizim, where the Samaritans had worshiped in their own temple for centuries, and to the other side at Mount Ebal, where Joshua had built an altar. A Samaritan woman walked up, ready to draw water for herself.

In a world of mutual bigotry, Jesus asked for a drink of water. The woman replied defensively, "Why do you, a Jewish man, ask for something to drink from me, a Samaritan woman?" (John 4:9).

Jesus said, "If you recognized God's gift and who is saying to you, 'Give me some water to drink,' you would be asking him, and he would give you living water" (4:10). Her answer was totally beside the point. She was dying in a material world; she had no understanding of the spiritual. She said, in effect, "Mister, I walk from the village two miles here and two miles back every day. If you have a better way so I don't have to carry water, I'd like to know about it."

Jesus pushed toward life issues: "Go, get your husband" (4:16). She answered that she had no husband. Jesus complimented her, saying, in effect, "You have told the truth."

Did you ever wonder why this woman came to the well at noon? All the other women of the village came in the cool of the evening, earthenware pots on their heads, to visit, to laugh, to exchange village gossip, to get water for the coming day. This woman came to the well in the heat of the day before the other women had come. She was isolated, cut off, estranged even in her own village. She was dying of loneliness.

Jesus said simply, "I Am—the one who speaks with you" (4:26). At that moment, the miracle of life came to her. She put down her jar and ran into town, crying out with joy, "Come and see a man who has told me everything I've done!" (4:29).

Now the witness of John's Gospel bubbles with excitement. "The Son gives life to whomever he wishes" (5:21). "Whoever hears my word and believes in the one who sent me has eternal life" (5:24).

John 3:16 has been called the gospel in miniature: "God so loved the world that he gave his only Son, so that everyone who believes in him won't perish but will have eternal life." Right here and now, a foreigner, a female, and a failure can drink the water of eternal life.

Sin and Suffering

All through our study we have struggled with the relationship between sin and suffering, illness and wrongdoing, injury and punishment. We know from experience and from studying the Bible that sin has devastating effects. But in Jesus' time as in Job's time, it was thought that accident, injury, and illness were all caused by sin. Sometimes Jesus related sin and sickness. When he healed the man who had been ill for thirty-eight years, Jesus said, "See! You have been made well. Don't sin anymore, in case something worse happens to you" (John 5:14).

But at other times there was no explanation. Just as God gave Job no answer, so Jesus did not explain. But he did clearly separate sin from many tragedies.

In every time of suffering there is a decision to be made that results in either bitterness or trust. The suffering of others can also cause us to minister to them out of love (doing the work of Jesus) and to turn from our sins lest worse things befall us.

NOTES

NOTES

Conflict With Unbelievers

We have emphasized new life, light (sight), and healing action. But John's Gospel also shows Jesus encountering spiritual blindness and death.

The blindness was rampant. Physical circumcision was not enough. As the prophets had said, salvation would require a circumcised heart. "This is the basis for judgment: The light came into the world, and people loved darkness rather than the light, for their actions are evil" (3:19).

The Prologue

Now we are ready to understand the Prologue of John (John 1:1-18). Jesus is the Word, spoken by the Father. Just as God spoke the Word in Creation, so God speaks now in the Son. The same creative energy and love that formed the universe now has become flesh. God is, in Jesus Christ, restoring the entire creation.

Foot Washing

Only John records the washing of the disciples' feet. This powerful symbolic act is set amid controversy, strife, and tension. Outside the room, forces are at work to destroy Jesus. Inside the room, Judas in his heart has already betrayed him. And according to Luke the disciples are arguing over who will be greatest in the Kingdom (Luke 22:24-27).

Common courtesy called for the host or servants to wash the dusty feet of the guests, as we today would open the door, hang up coats, offer a place to wash, give a cold drink. But the full significance of Jesus' act of love in this everyday courtesy, no doubt, did not become apparent to his disciples until after his crucifixion.

Jesus continually showed his disciples that the Son of Man came to serve and called his disciples to serve also (John 13:1-15). He made his actions clear with his words: Those greatest in the Kingdom are those who serve.

As disciples, you too will be asked to give humble service rather than to seek high honor.

The Promise of the Holy Spirit

The Gospels often refer to the Spirit. John the Baptist said, "I baptize you with water, but he will baptize you with the Holy Spirit" (Mark 1:8). The Holy Spirit came upon Jesus at baptism "like a dove" (1:10). Luke recorded, "If you who are evil know how to give good gifts to your children, how much more will the heavenly Father give the Holy Spirit to those who ask him!" (Luke 11:13).

Now in John's Gospel, Jesus offers the Holy Spirit, who is Comforter, Counselor, Advocate. This same Holy Spirit is the Spirit of truth (later in Paul's writings referred to as the Spirit of Jesus Christ). The Spirit will help disciples walk the way, for Jesus now proclaims himself as "the way, the truth, and the life" (John 14:6).

Disciples will do even greater things than Jesus did in his earthly ministry (14:12). Why? Because Jesus will go to the Father and because the Father will send the Holy Spirit (Advocate) "who will be with you forever" (14:16).

The Lamb

John the Baptist, when he saw Jesus, cried out, "Look! The Lamb of God who takes away the sin of the world!" (John 1:29). After the Crucifixion and Resurrection, after Jesus offered himself as a sacrifice, a slain lamb, the disciples, guided by the Spirit, must have thought, "O dear God, that is what John the Baptist meant when he said, 'Here is the Lamb of God.'"

In John 15, the disciples are moving into a new level of intimacy with Jesus. He has been Rabbi, Son of Man, Son of God, Messiah. But now fresh spiritual intertwining emerges: "I am the vine; you are the branches" (15:5).

Recall that in Matthew, Mark, and Luke, Jesus was training disciples to do the very works of compassion and conversion that he did. Now in John, with the coming of the Advocate, they will be empowered to do those works. The fruit will grow on the vine if the branches flow with the Word and Spirit.

Last-Minute Instructions

"I didn't say these things to you from the beginning, because I was with you. . . . If I don't go away, the Companion won't come to you. But if I go, I will send him to you. When he comes, he will show the world it was wrong about sin, righteousness, and judgment" (John 16:4-8). We know and understand Jesus Christ now, enlightened by the Spirit. Even the apostles did not comprehend until the Holy Spirit opened their eyes: Times will be tough. You will be driven from the synagogues, scattered, killed. But the promise matches the times. "In the world you have distress. But be encouraged! I have conquered the world" (16:33). What does that mean? That you will have no trouble? No. It means rejoice even in suffering because the final victory belongs to God (see Romans 8:31-39).

Jesus Prays

Jesus' prayer in John 17 is called the high priestly prayer because in it Jesus consecrated himself as the one perfect sacrifice for the sins of the world and then consecrated his disciples for service to win the world for God.

Christian believers are set apart to serve. But they are not to be isolated. "I am not asking that you take them out of the world but that you keep then safe from the evil one. . . . As you sent me into the world, so I have sent them into the world" (17:15-18). And so Jesus prays that they may be equipped for the work to which they are sent.

The Passion in John

In John, the experience in Gethsemane focuses on the betrayal and arrest. Notice that Peter was ill-prepared to meet the crisis. He was confused by the foot washing, angry enough to cut off a slave's ear during the arrest, and full of denials and curses when asked if he was one of the disciples.

Two thoughts on the Resurrection: Mary did not recognize Jesus at first. His was not a resuscitated body but a resurrected body. "Don't hold on to me, for I haven't yet gone up to my Father" (20:17). But notice the powerful point. Mary Magdalene recognized Jesus when he called her by name. God always calls people by name, for we are God's children, "the sheep of his pasture." We know God is alive when he calls us by name.

Also, just as Matthew records the Great Commission, "Go and make disciples" (Matthew 28:19), John records a similar sending forth: " 'As the Father sent me, so I am sending you.' Then he breathed on them and said, 'Receive the Holy Spirit. If you forgive anyone's sins, they are forgiven; if you don't forgive them, they aren't forgiven' " (John 20:21-23). We know God is alive when the Almighty breathes the spirit of mission into us.

MARKS OF DISCIPLESHIP

For John, a disciple is one who has found light in a blind and darkened world, spiritual food and drink in a hungry and thirsty world, meaning in a confusing and seemingly meaningless world, direction and community in a lost and lonely world.

Try, in your own words, to describe the "life" you have found in Jesus Christ.

Mark of Discipleship
Disciples experience life in Jesus Christ and have the inner assurance of abundant, eternal life.

The Christian doctrine of "assurance," or inward witness, means that Christians can know in their heart that they are loved and have life, abundant and eternal.

We have three testimonies that disciples are the children of God: the Spirit, the water of Jesus' baptism, and the blood of Christ. All three agree and give us our assurance (1 John 5:6-12).

In a world of sham and superficiality where much religion is form, as a disciple, are you able to say, "I know the one in whom I've placed my trust. I'm convinced that God is powerful enough to protect what he has placed in my trust until that day" (2 Timothy 1:12)?

Do you have a sense of assurance? How would you describe your feelings?

What meaning, what purpose does your life have in Christ?

IF YOU WANT TO KNOW MORE

One of the early heresies in the church was the Marcion heresy. It basically rejected the Old Testament and regarded the world as evil. Jesus was "spiritual," not physical; he only seemed to be human. Look up *Marcion* and compare his ideas with what John's Gospel says about Jesus. Also read the Apostles' Creed. Notice how it rejects the Marcion heresy.

John uses many symbols and descriptive contrasts to interpret Jesus Christ to his readers. Each symbol presents a little different picture of who Christ is and the meaning he brings to the life of those who receive him. As you read the Gospel of John, make a list of those symbols and contrasts, where they are found, and how they translate into meaning for today's seeker.

Did you wonder what happened to Nicodemus? Look up the three instances where he is mentioned in John (3:1-21; 7:45-52; 19:38-42). How would you describe his form of discipleship?

Look up the word *Incarnation.* What does it mean? Look up *fellowship (koinonia).* Confession, as in 1 John 1:9, was practiced in the Christian fellowship for several centuries and continues to be practiced today in the Roman Catholic Church. How deep a level of pain and guilt are you able to share within your DISCIPLE group? Do you have someone to whom you can make confession and feel clean inside?

"Rather, you will receive power when the Holy Spirit has come upon you, and you will be my witnesses in Jerusalem, in all Judea and Samaria, and to the end of the earth."
—Acts 1:8

5 The Explosive Power of the Spirit

OUR HUMAN CONDITION

We believe in God, but we have so little power. We want to witness, to heal, to convert nonbelievers, to serve, to change society; but we are ordinary people. We lack spiritual vitality.

ASSIGNMENT

In some ways, it is too bad Acts does not follow Luke, as they were written as two volumes of one work. Luke recorded the ministry of Jesus Christ, and Acts witnessed to the work of the early church. Still, there were powerful reasons for putting the three Synoptic Gospels together and then John as the fourth Gospel. Matthew, Mark, and Luke take similar approaches to telling the story of the life and mission of Jesus and have much of the same material. However, John concentrates on presenting Jesus as the Messiah and contains material that the other three Gospels do not.

Glance back at the end of Luke before you begin reading Acts.

Pray daily before study:

"Let God grant us grace and bless us;
   let God make his face shine on us,
   so that your way becomes known
      on earth,
   so that your salvation becomes known
      among all the nations" (Psalm 67:1-2).

Prayer concerns for the week:

Betty Chaussweller
Melanie Iverson
Lynn Jordan
Donna Merril
Jane Shirk
Betty Hayes
Mary Iverson

Day 1 **Read Acts 1–3** (Pentecost, healing a man who is crippled).

What is a Sabbath Day's walk?
Sun turned to darkness, moon to blood.

The Case for Christ.

Day 2 **Read Acts 4–6** (boldness of Peter and John, Ananias and Sapphira, Stephen's arrest).

Day 3 **Read Acts 7–9** (Stephen's martyrdom, Philip and the Ethiopian eunuch, Saul's conversion).

Day 4 **Read Acts 10–12** (Cornelius, James killed, Peter imprisoned and freed).

Day 5 **Read Acts 13–15:35** (Paul and Barnabas as missionaries).

Day 6 **Read "The Bible Teaching" and the "Marks of Discipleship" and answer the questions.**

Day 7 **Rest, pray, and attend class.**

THE BIBLE TEACHING

Acts falls naturally into two parts: The first concentrates on the early church in and near Jerusalem and the second on Paul and his mission enterprises. Acts traces the spread of the church from Jerusalem to Rome. Like the waves made when a stone is thrown into a lake, the witness of the church moves out in concentric circles until it reaches the distant shores.

Acts could be titled the Acts of the Holy Spirit in the Early Church. The writer of Acts was looking back, amazed at the church's Spirit-directed history. As we read, we sense the wonder that there was a church at all, but believers knew the church existed by the activity of God.

The author of Acts is thought to have been a Gentile physician named Luke who was often a companion of Paul. Luke is mentioned in Colossians 4:14 and 2 Timothy 4:11.

Pentecost

Every community needs to remember its beginning, for that in part defines what the community becomes. So we sometimes say that Pentecost is the birthday of the church. But the birthday comparison is only partly true. Certainly there was a new, powerful burst of faith and zeal, but the community of faith reached backward into Israel, back to Abraham and Sarah. It also strained forward in messianic expectation.

Jesus taught clearly that the Holy Spirit would come to all the believers, not just to the Twelve. "You will receive power [*dunamis*—the root word of *dynamic, dynamite*] when the Holy Spirit has come upon you" (Acts 1:8).

So they waited patiently in the upper room. "All [the eleven disciples] were united in their devotion to prayer, along with some women, including Mary the mother of Jesus, and his brothers" (1:14). Note the sense of unity and harmony among men and women, family and friends, apostles and other believers. Unity is reemphasized in 2:1: "When Pentecost Day arrived, they were all together in one place."

Pentecost, the festival of first fruits fifty days after Passover, was a Jewish holy day. Now Christians celebrate Pentecost fifty days after Easter to recall the explosive power of the Spirit that launched the Christian community into mission.

How do you describe a dramatic religious experience? Luke used imagery: a sound "like the howling of a fierce wind" and "individual flames of fire" (Acts 2:2-3). Then people began to speak in various languages, seemingly in the languages of the nations of the world. The tower of Babel was reversed. Sin destroyed communication; the Holy Spirit restored communication. The experience was not primarily *glossolalia*, speaking in unknown tongues. Rather, it was a missionary propulsion, dynamically thrusting the believers into a worldwide ministry.

They were ecstatic but not drunk; it was "only nine o'clock in the morning" (2:15). Peter, who had sworn he had never heard of Jesus during the trial, now stood up in the main street of Jerusalem and preached. The power had come.

Peter began by quoting the prophet Joel, who had called for repentance, "for the day of the LORD is coming" (Joel 2:1). Joel's words have certain apocalyptic overtones: End times are coming; repent. Peter said it was happening as Joel had said (Acts 2:16-21).

Then Peter proclaimed Jesus crucified and raised from the dead. The listeners "were deeply troubled" and asked, "What should we do?" (2:37). Peter's answer, and our answer to people who are receptive to God, is, "Change your hearts and lives. Each of you must be baptized in the name of Jesus Christ for the forgiveness of your sins. Then you will receive the gift of the Holy Spirit" (2:38). Three thousand people were baptized.

But watch! They were immediately gathered into house groups. Since they had no churches, they met in one another's homes, almost daily. Look carefully at what they did. "The believers devoted themselves to the apostles' teaching, to the community, to their shared meals, and to their prayers" (2:42). Today we might say they studied the Scriptures, shared one another's lives (*koinonia,* fellowship, community), broke bread both in refreshment and in the Lord's Supper, and prayed together.

Wonders and signs of the Kingdom occurred. Instead of being selfish, they shared with one another and gave to the needy. They went to the Temple, kept the Sabbath, and daily went in and out of one another's homes praising God. Then this glorious verse: "The Lord added daily to the community those who were being saved" (2:47).

Now what Jesus had promised was happening: Disciples would perform signs of the Kingdom as he had. Peter and John healed a man lame from birth (3:1-10). The healing became an opportunity for witnessing and a call to repentance (3:11-26). Peter and the others showed boldness again, for "the apostles were teaching the people and announcing that the resurrection of the dead was happening because of Jesus" (4:2). Peter and John were in trouble because the Sadducees did not teach belief in resurrection. But empowered now by the Holy Spirit, Peter and John continued to act and speak boldly: "We can't stop speaking about what we have seen and heard" (4:20). When the church rejoiced over Peter and John's release from custody, they sang or chanted Psalm 2, interpreting it now as their own (4:25-26).

The people were no longer merely tithers. Now they were free from anxiety over "what you'll eat or what you'll drink, . . . what you'll wear" (Matthew 6:25). They gave to one another and to the common treasury. Then Barnabas, one of the greatest servants of the church, appeared. His given name was Joseph, but the apostles gave him the name "one who encourages" (Acts 4:36). He was a direct descendant of the tribe of Levi and lived in Cyprus among Gentiles, so he spoke Greek. He sold his field and put the total proceeds in the care of the apostles (4:36-37). Persons have done such from time to time across the centuries; and when they do, the church explodes with new vitality.

You will observe later that Barnabas was responsible for nurturing Paul, letting him take leadership, giving him encouragement, and working constantly for the inclusion of Gentile converts in the church. When the break between Barnabas and Paul came over a dispute concerning John Mark, Barnabas took John Mark and began nurturing him.

Now, in deliberate contrast, Ananias and Sapphira sold their land and gave only a part of the proceeds into the apostles' care (5:1-11). Was the issue money? No. They did not need to give anything. Then why were they confronted so dramatically by Peter and the Holy Spirit? Because they lied! The church could not tolerate deception. A lie will bring down a family, a church, a business, even a government. The newly formed Christian community was so transparent, so open with one another, so filled with giving and joy, so honest with one another that all kinds of healings and forgiveness and conversions were taking place. Now came "Adam and Eve" wanting to have their apple and eat it too. Peter rightly said, "They will carry you out" (5:9), for either they died, or the church died.

Stephen

People, not angels, make up the church. The church is imperfect disciples in the process of becoming like Jesus. Members of the early community of faith shared with one another and took care of the needy. Widows were of particular concern. But some members were native Judeans who spoke Aramaic and had traditionally resisted Greek language and culture. Others were Hellenists, Jews who had lived in different parts of the world and who spoke Greek. Barnabas and Saul were Hellenist Jews. So was Stephen.

Whoever was providing food for the widows seemed to be favoring the Judean Jews. The "daily manna" was not evenly distributed. The Twelve (Judas had been replaced by Matthias in Acts 1:15-26) called the body together and acted to reduce the tension.

The apostles needed to be consumed with prayer, preaching, and teaching the word. So the problem was placed in the hands of others.

The community selected seven persons to serve tables, men who were filled with the Spirit and had good reputations. Notice that all seven were Hellenists; that is, they were from the group doing the complaining. Do you remember Jethro's advice to Moses about spreading the labor (Exodus 18:13-27)?

When these seven were chosen and harmony restored, "God's word continued to grow. The number of disciples in Jerusalem increased significantly" (Acts 6:7).

Stephen was the first of the Christian martyrs. (The word *martyr* means witness.) He was so filled with the Spirit that he began to witness as well as wait tables. His sermon retraced Hebrew history, seeing it through "Resurrection glasses." Like the prophets, he accused his hearers, "You stubborn people! In your thoughts and hearing, you are like those who have had no part in God's covenant! You continuously set yourself against the Holy Spirit, just like your ancestors did" (7:51). When he looked to heaven and declared that he saw "the Human One standing at God's right side" (7:56), the council members were furious. They violated Roman law, which did not allow the religious council to carry out a death sentence on its own authority, and stoned Stephen to death (7:58). Stephen's prayer echoed the prayers of Jesus: "Lord Jesus, accept my life!" (Acts 7:59; see Luke 23:46) and "Lord, don't hold this sin against them!" (Acts 7:60; see Luke 23:34).

Saul (Paul)

As you now encounter Saul (Paul) in Acts 7:58 and 8:1, answer the following questions using Acts 22:3-16; 26:9-18 and Galatians 1:13-17 to help you.

What was Saul's background?

Why might Saul seem to be the least likely candidate for a missionary?

What seemingly negative characteristics in Paul became "positives" in his work as a missionary?

Gentiles

If Christianity was to become more than a Jewish sect, it had to break loose among the Gentiles. Luke, writing in Acts, showed the groundswell of activity as the Holy Spirit moved among the disciples. Thousands of people were becoming Christians. Some were selected for the Acts account.

Why do you think Luke recorded Philip's conversion of the Ethiopian eunuch (Acts 8:26-39)?

What did Peter's vision at Joppa mean (Acts 10:9-16)?

A church-shaping crisis, indeed a world-shaping crisis, arose over the mission to the Gentiles. An apostolic conference was called in Jerusalem (Acts 15). Conservative Judean Jews wanted to require all Gentiles who converted to Christianity to follow Jewish laws, including food laws and circumcision. The Hellenist Jews, such as Barnabas and Paul disagreed.

Peter, a Judean Jew, leaning toward the conservative side, nevertheless had his strange vision in Joppa. James, the brother of Jesus, also in touch with the conservatives, made the great compromise not to include circumcision.

Notice—and this was Paul and Barnabas's great point—that the council's decision did not require circumcision. But certain other restrictions were retained.

MARKS OF DISCIPLESHIP

Being a disciple calls for both active and passive responses. Sometimes Jesus requires us to get up and do something: "Come, follow me" (Mark 10:21). Sometimes Jesus requires us to wait and pray: "Stay in the city until you have been furnished with heavenly power" (Luke 24:49). Remember that Jesus began his ministry by receiving the Holy Spirit in baptism and by waiting forty days in fasting and prayer. Too often we who are individualists and activists do not wait and pray together to receive the power.

NOTES

Mark of Discipleship
Disciples experience the presence and the power of the Holy Spirit in their lives and witness to others in order to lead them to Jesus.

What sense do you have of the presence and power of the Holy Spirit in your life?

What about your church? How are healing, witnessing, serving, and rebirth occurring in the congregation?

Do your group members ever pray that the Holy Spirit will empower them to help revitalize the congregation?

As Protestant or Roman Catholic Christians, we have some traditions that are precious to us, as did the Judean Jewish Christians. Some we can yield in order to receive "outsiders" as converts; others we cannot. What traditions could we yield?

What are some beliefs or practices we must insist on?

IF YOU WANT TO KNOW MORE

The Bible does not dwell on martyrdom, although countless Christians, even very early, were persecuted, imprisoned, and killed. Look up *martyr* or *persecution* in a Bible dictionary.

"You know I have testified to both Jews and Greeks that they must change their hearts and lives as they turn to God and have faith in our Lord Jesus." —Acts 20:21

6 The Gospel Penetrates the World

OUR HUMAN CONDITION

We are uncomfortable witnessing about our faith to strangers and people of different religions. Even with our families and next-door neighbors we hesitate to talk about God. We suspect that people will resent ideas that challenge their beliefs or customs. Besides, we're not sure we would want them to join us.

ASSIGNMENT

The church with its gospel of Jesus Christ continues to expand across the Mediterranean world and to Rome. If your Bible has maps, take time to locate the cities or areas about which you are reading. Observe the adaptability of the gospel in the many settings in which it is proclaimed.

Pray daily before study:

"But me? I will sing of your strength!
  In the morning I will shout out loud
  about your faithful love
    because you have been my
      stronghold,
    my shelter when I was distraught.
I will sing praises to you, my strength,
  because God is my stronghold,
  my loving God" (Psalm 59:16-17).

Prayer concerns for the week:

Susan Byrd
Mary Iverson
Lynn Jordan

Day 1 **Read Acts 15:36–18** (Paul goes to Macedonia, preaches at Athens and Corinth).

Day 2 **Read Acts 19–20** (Paul at Ephesus); **Ephesians 1–4** (love surpassing knowledge, grace).

Riot in Ephesus. Silversmith were angry because Paul said that the idols they were crafting were not gods. (Artemis) Paul goes to Macedonia + Greece Eutychus raised from the dead at Troas. Ep. Christ is to put into effect to be holy and blameless in his sight.

Day 3 **Read Acts 21–23** (return to Jerusalem, arrest, Paul's defense before the council).

Day 4 **Read Acts 24–26** (Paul's appeal to Caesar, defense before Agrippa).

Day 5 **Read Acts 27–28** (storm and shipwreck on the way to Rome).

Day 6 Read "The Bible Teaching" and the "Marks of Discipleship" and answer the questions.

Day 7 Rest, pray, and attend class.

DISCIPLE FAST TRACK

THE BIBLE TEACHING

The powerful personality of Paul, driven by the Holy Spirit, dominates the remainder of Acts. Through Paul's missionary activity and the work of countless others, the gospel moved by foot, by horseback, by ship all over the known world. The Greek language was spoken widely, and Roman roads and Roman peace made travel easier than it had ever been.

Jewish communities and synagogues existed almost everywhere; so traveling Jews, even if they were Jewish Christians, were, at least at first, given Jewish hospitality.

As a result of such internal motivation and external opportunity, the gospel went worldwide. Paul led the way. Hosts of others, including the apostles, scattered out. Persecution, at first in Jerusalem and later elsewhere, caused believers to hurry from one place to another. They scattered as wind scatters a prairie fire.

Early on, the team was Barnabas and Paul, as the "son of encouragement" nurtured the young Pharisee Christian. Soon, however, it became Paul and Barnabas, as Paul's driving leadership took over. Then a breach occurred that served the cause well (Acts 15:36-41). Barnabas wanted to take along John Mark, his nephew. Paul refused, for the lad had been homesick and had left them on an earlier trip. The solution was for Paul and Barnabas to separate. Barnabas and John Mark went to Cyprus, Paul and Silas to Asia Minor.

Usually Paul and his companions would enter a city as they did Philippi: "We stayed in this city several days. On the Sabbath we went outside the city gate to the riverbank, where we thought there might be a place for prayer. We sat down and began to talk to the women who had gathered" (16:12-13). For centuries now, Jews in various towns and cities had gathered in Sabbath groupings, often at the riverside. Such a gathering was an informal synagogue without a building, a place to sing psalms, offer prayers, study and discuss the Scriptures, and remember who they were. Some who attended were God-fearers, Gentiles who were attracted to worship of the one true God.

Lydia, a traveling merchant and a Gentile God-fearer, was converted and baptized along with her household. She insisted that Paul and Silas stay in her home.

In Thessalonica there was a regular synagogue. According to his usual custom, Paul went to the synagogue. (Had not Jesus said the gospel came first to the Jews?) There, he "for three Sabbaths interacted with them on the basis of the scriptures. Through his interpretation of the scriptures, he demonstrated that the Christ had to suffer and rise from the dead" (17:2-3). Remember, "scriptures" at this time meant the Hebrew Scriptures. None of the New Testament had yet been written. Again people were converted—a few Jews and "a larger number of Greek God-worshippers and quite a few prominent women" (17:4).

In Athens Paul spoke in the city council, the Areopagus, where philosophers loved to gather and talk (17:22-31). Paul had little effect, but a few believed.

In Corinth Paul had great success. Corinth was a bustling seaport city filled with people from all over the world—sailors, shippers, merchants, slaves, prostitutes, Romans, Greeks, Jews. It was a melting pot, though many considered it a cesspool. The temple of Aphrodite was there with its one thousand sacred prostitutes. What a place to start a church!

At Corinth Paul stayed with Priscilla and her husband, Aquila. They were tentmakers by trade; so was Paul. (The Common English Bible says they "worked with leather" [18:3].) Thus Paul used both his occupation and his relationship with a Jewish family to begin his work. "Every Sabbath he interacted with people in the synagogue, trying to convince both Jews and Greeks" (18:4).

Notice that Paul used everything to make converts: his Jewish heritage, his Greek language, his tentmaking (leatherworking) skills, his training in Torah, and now his Roman citizenship. He wrote to the Corinthian church, "I have become all things to all people, so I could save some by all possible means" (1 Corinthians 9:22; read 9:19-23).

When you read Paul's defenses in his trials, you learn a lot about him, but you also learn a lot about Jesus. Paul used the court proceedings as a chance to convert. King Agrippa, distinguished and experienced, interrupted, "Are you trying to convince me that, in such a short time, you've made me a Christian?" (Acts 26:28).

Paul was a Roman citizen. To hold the coveted Roman citizenship, one could be born a free Roman citizen, buy Roman citizenship, or receive citizenship as an honor for military or civil service to the empire. We do not know how Paul's (Saul's) father became a Roman citizen, but we know Paul was proud to have been born a Roman citizen.

Why did he finally appeal to his rights as a Roman citizen? Did he miscalculate? Agrippa said to Festus in Caesarea, "This man could have been released if he hadn't appealed to Caesar" (26:32). Was he weary of two years of harassment and jail? Or did he want to carry the gospel to Spain by way of Rome? One suspects that the symbolism of going to the heart of the empire and to the end of the world (Spain) was a powerful motive. Paul did not make it to Spain; but his witness in and to Rome, his letters to the churches while in prison in Rome, and his eventual martyrdom in Rome made the Christian movement international.

In the closing verses of Acts, Luke is saying something about the providence of God. Paul, sent to Rome by the anger of a dozen cities, enjoyed the greatest opportunity of his career to offer to others abundant and eternal life. "Paul lived in his own rented quarters [under house arrest in Rome] for two full years and welcomed everyone who came to him. Unhindered and with complete confidence, he continued to preach God's kingdom and to teach about the Lord Jesus Christ" (28:30-31).

Acts tells us that Paul spent more time in Ephesus than anywhere else. Read Paul's letter to the Ephesian Christians, as it provides a good summary of Paul's understanding of Christian thinking and living. The following brief summary is a good introduction to this letter.

The Letter to the Ephesians

Ephesians is a letter to all the churches, not just to the church at Ephesus. Converts are not won to be individual, solitary, saved souls. No, God is forming the new humanity, the new harmony of people, which was, after all, God's original plan. "God destined us to be his adopted children through Jesus Christ" (Ephesians 1:5). God is working to remove all the disharmonies of the universe. In the midst of a world speaking countless languages (and hating one another), Christ is breaking down barriers and building unity.

In Ephesians, it is whispered as a secret. No one suspects. No one but the believers know. "God revealed his hidden design to us, which is according to his goodwill. . . . God planned for the climax of all times: to bring all things together in Christ, the things in heaven along with the things on earth" (1:9-10).

How is God going to do this? In an unbelievable way—by the blood of Jesus. In the Bible, the blood of Jesus refers to the entire outpouring of Christ's love, from the beginning to the end, but particularly at Calvary.

Paul had seen the power of Christ's love overcome impossible divisions among people. He had seen Samaritans and Jews praying together, Gentiles and Jews breaking bread together, men and women working and worshiping together. At the foot of the cross, Persians and Romans and Greeks and Judean Jews and free people and slaves were on their knees together.

"Christ is our peace. He made both Jews and Gentiles into one group. With his body, he broke down the barrier of hatred that divided us. He canceled the detailed rules of the Law so that he could create one new person out of the two groups, making peace. He reconciled them both as one body to God by the cross, which ended the hostility to God" (2:14-16). The blood of Christ will bring us all together. To that mission, Paul gave his life.

MARKS OF DISCIPLESHIP

Disciples are to be witnesses. Paul used everything he had to bring men and women to God, every relationship, every aspect of background or culture. What do you have to offer that could help you relate to other people in witness and converting power? To what ethnic group do you belong? What languages do you speak? Are you young? old? married? single? rural? urban? poor? rich? Are you a former alcoholic? Have you ever been fired from a job? divorced? a fraternity or sorority member? a school dropout? What is your faith experience?

NOTES

Mark of Discipleship
Disciples witness to others in order to lead them to Jesus Christ.

Who are you? Think of ways you could use who you are and your experience to help lead people to Christ Jesus.

Ephesians declares that Jew and Gentile are brought together in Christ. Do you see harmony developing in your Christian fellowship? Are you willing to test it further, extending it to persons of other cultures, age groups, social strata? If that is what God is trying to do through Christ, how can you work with Christ?

IF YOU WANT TO KNOW MORE

To get a sense of the points and sources of unity among Christians, go as a group or as individuals to a worship service in a Protestant, Roman Catholic, or Orthodox congregation different from yours. Describe your experience.

Most of us remember ideas, events, or times when we know something about the people involved. Look up information and write a sentence or two about Timothy, John Mark, Lydia, Apollos, Silas, King Agrippa, Priscilla and Aquila, and Luke.

"Therefore, since we are justified by faith, we have peace with God through our Lord Jesus Christ." —Romans 5:1, NRSV

7 Put Right With God Through Faith

OUR HUMAN CONDITION

Part of the time we deliberately rebel. We do what we please. We go directly against God. But part of the time we "religious people" work hard to win God's approval, only to fail. We lack peace within ourselves and with others.

ASSIGNMENT

The importance of Romans to the early church is indicated by its position in the New Testament. It is placed first among Paul's letters, even though Paul had written other letters earlier. Content and length rather than age, no doubt, influenced its location in the canon.

Pray daily before study:

> "Your loyal love, LORD extends to the
>   skies;
>   your faithfulness reaches the clouds.
> Your righteousness is like the strongest
>   mountains;
>   your justice is like the deepest sea"
>   (Psalm 36:5-6).

Prayer concerns for the week:

Day 1 **Read Romans 1–4** (Jews and Gentiles under judgment).

Day 4 **Read Romans 11–13** (salvation for Israel and Gentiles, the wild olive grafted in).

Day 2 **Read Romans 5–7** (righteous through faith).

Day 5 **Read Romans 14–16** (life in the body of Christ, the strong and the weak).

Day 3 **Read Romans 8–10** (Adam and Christ, law and sin, life in the Spirit).

Day 6 **Read "The Bible Teaching" and the "Marks of Discipleship" and answer the questions.**

Day 7 **Rest, pray, and attend class.**

THE BIBLE TEACHING

When Paul wrote Romans, he was no longer a fledgling missionary. He was at the height of his powers, disciplined by torture, sharpened by prayer and preaching, able to state the Christian faith with clarity and persuasive power. Paul wrote to the Romans from Corinth, where he was teaching in the Corinthian church, collecting money for the poor in Jerusalem, and dreaming of going to Rome and to Spain to encourage the church everywhere.

Martin Luther called Romans "the chief part of the New Testament," saying that it contains "the very purest gospel." It has often brought revival to the church; and it profoundly influenced Luther, Augustine, John Calvin, John Wesley, and Karl Barth. Many would say it is the most important theological book ever written.

Sin and Justification

To understand Paul's Letter to the Romans, we first must remember Genesis 1–11. To comprehend the height of our salvation, we must know the depth of our sin.

Paul recalls that we do not merely do bad things; we are out of harmony with God. As Adam and Eve and King Saul were disobedient, so we are disobedient. As Cain and King David were passionately rebellious, so we are passionately rebellious. As King Solomon and those who built the tower of Babel were arrogant and proud, so we are arrogant and proud.

The Gentiles have no excuse, wrote Paul, because just looking at the universe should have revealed the true nature of the great and glorious Creator. All of us, even the Gentiles, have a conscience, know right from wrong, and know there is God. We all stand condemned.

The Jews were given the law of Moses, but they did not keep it. The Law in fact showed their sin the way a plumb line shows a crooked wall. Further, many Jews indulged in the very things they condemned in the Gentiles. Their hearts were proud and stubborn; they were self-centered, wrote Paul.

The net result is that all women and all men, the Gentile with the law of conscience, the Jew with the law of Moses, are sinners. Paul insists, "Those who have sinned outside the Law will also die outside the Law, and those who have sinned under the Law will be judged by the Law" (Romans 2:12). He therefore quotes the psalmist:

> "There is no righteous person,
>   not even one; . . . .
> They all turned away.
>   They have become worthless together"
>   (Romans 3:10-12; see Psalm 14:1-3).

Sin turns us in a downward spiral. First we exchange the truth about God for a lie and worship and serve the creation rather than the creator (Romans 1:25). Then when we live in twisted relationships, God gives us up to the passions of our hearts. Out of a polluted well comes polluted water. Paul lists the terrible results of corrupt thinking and acting through which we humans destroy one another. Our lives deteriorate until finally we not only do evil deeds but approve others who do evil (1:32).

God had to act. We could not extract ourselves from enslavement to self-centeredness. The disease was too rampant, the separation too severe, the spiritual relationship too strained. We were helpless. God had to act.

Jesus has made a breakthrough for us. Paul tries to explain it. He uses the word *redemption* (3:24, NRSV). Redemption was used for slaves. Slaves could be bought and set free. "You have been bought and paid for," wrote Paul (1 Corinthians 6:20).

When the Hebrews were slaves in Egypt, God "redeemed" his people from slavery. Hosea redeemed his wife by paying the price of a slave and setting her free to be his wife again. Jesus Christ redeems sinners.

To whom or what have we become enslaved? To our own self-interest? Yes, and more, to that passionate disobedience that we call sin. The result of that enslavement is doom. But we have been bought and set free.

A phrase Paul uses is *the place of sacrifice where mercy is found by means of his blood* (Romans 3:25). Just as the blood of the sacrificed lamb was sprinkled on the doorposts of the Hebrews in Egypt in order that death would not destroy the firstborn of God's people, so the blood of Christ has been sprinkled on the doorposts of our hearts so that evil will not destroy us. Divine wrath will pass over God's people.

Study Romans 3:21-26 carefully and rewrite the passage in your own words.

Another phrase Paul uses is Christ's *righteous act of one person* (5:18). Paul understood that Jesus did something no one else in all history had ever done: He lived his life in right relationship with the Father. Amid a fractured humanity Jesus said, "I and the Father are one" (John 10:30). Jesus did something the whole of humankind had been waiting for: He lived the obedient life, right to the final words on the cross, "It is completed" (John 19:30). With Christ's act of obedience, he broke a hole in the enemy's lines so that his followers could walk through.

Perhaps the most helpful word Paul uses is *justify* (Romans 5:1, 9, NRSV). God justifies us, puts us right, in Jesus Christ. Any printer would know what the word means. Historically a printer, after setting the type, needed to "justify," or adjust, the page. A modern word processor has a built-in justifier. A person types in the letters, but the machine "justifies," that is, it spaces letters properly and establishes margins so that the material is in right relationship. To be righteous does not mean to be "pure" or "good" but rather to be in harmony, in right relationship, both with God and with neighbor.

When a person accepts this work of God in faith, a kind of death occurs, the death of self-centeredness. Burial by baptism symbolizes that death. A resurrection occurs as we stand up from baptism with a new master, bought with a price, passed over because of his blood, and justified into right relationship with the Creator of the universe.

Abraham trusted in God even before he was circumcised. *"Abraham had faith in God, and it was credited to him as righteousness"* (Romans 4:3, quoting Genesis 15:6). The circumcision was *sign* of the covenant, not source. So we Gentiles in Jesus Christ are grafted into God's true people by faith. We now, with the Hebrew ancestors, walk into the future unafraid, as children of the covenant. We are blessed, ready to be used as a blessing to the world.

Grace, accepted by faith, makes us sons and daughters of God. That is what God wanted all along, not robots, but not rebels either. Since we are children of God, then we are heirs, able now to inherit everything God intended the children to have (Romans 8:14-17).

Now we know some things we never knew before:

- We know we have a new status.
- We understand that suffering can be a creative and positive force.
- We participate in a new humanity.
- No power in the universe can prevent our obtaining ultimate victory in Jesus Christ.

Restoration of Israel

Today some people wonder, "Should we dismiss the Old Testament and Judaism as irrelevant?" No. We in the Disciple study know that we cannot comprehend the gospel without its Old Testament roots.

How are we to think about the relationship of Jews to Jesus? Paul says their rejection of Jesus as the Messiah made the good news available to the Gentiles. God, who works for good in all things, used the crucifixion of Jesus to provide an atoning sacrifice for sin and used rejection by the Jews to open the door of salvation to the whole world.

Should we try to win Jews through our witness to grace? Yes, as we would try to win all people by our witness. But remember the Jews are our spiritual ancestors. Paul uses the metaphor of the olive tree to help us here. The branches of believing Gentiles (you and me) are grafted into the olive tree (Israel). Nonbelieving Jews are branches broken off. We who have been grafted in have no basis for pride; in fact, to show arrogance means God must prune us off too (compare John 15:1-11).

Will God save the chosen people? Yes. Paul says that when they see Gentiles becoming heirs of the promises made to Abraham, they will turn to Christ in faith. Thus God's plan for both Jews and Gentiles will be accomplished (Romans 11:11-32). Now in the new covenant we too are blessed to be a blessing.

Grace and Peace

Paul usually began his letters by offering grace and peace to his readers. Peace is that vibrant shalom that rings with harmony—being at one with God, with neighbor, and with self. The entire universe is groaning for the peace that characterized creation on the seventh day but was desecrated by the disobedience of humankind. Peace through Christ and his indwelling Spirit gives assurance to every Christian that all is well. Love casts out fear and brings perfect peace.

In that peace we know we are never alone, never defeated. We have the assurance that God cares for us and guides our ways. (Theologians call it providence.) "We know that God works all things together for good for the ones who love God" (Romans 8:28). What a sense of inner peace to trust that "nothing can separate us from God's love in Christ Jesus our Lord" (8:38).

Grace is the sacrificial, accepting, forgiving love of God expressed and revealed in Jesus. Paul always mentions it first, for grace is the source of our peace. Grace is love with no strings attached, poured forth in the total life and death and resurrection of Jesus. To be saved means to fling one's soul on that grace.

Christians sing,

> "Amazing grace! How sweet the sound
> that saved a wretch like me!"

This hymn was written by John Newton, a one-time slave trader, after his conversion. It expresses the joy of a person found by God's seeking love.

> "I once was lost, but now am found;
> was blind, but now I see."

MARKS OF DISCIPLESHIP

So often in Paul's letters, a *therefore* stands like a swinging door. Coming before the *therefore* is the mighty work of God in Jesus Christ. Moving from it is the awesome responsibility of Christian living. Like a slave set free by a benevolent master, we choose to serve out of love and gratitude.

Mark of Discipleship
Disciples receive and trust the forgiving love of God in Jesus Christ and serve out of love and gratitude.

"Therefore, since we have been made righteous through his faithfulness, we have peace with God through our Lord Jesus Christ" (Romans 5:1). "So, . . . present your bodies as a living sacrifice that is holy and pleasing to God" (12:1). We are saved by grace through faith. A claim is laid upon our lives. The forgiving love must be received. The work of God must be claimed by an act of trust.

Read Romans 12–15 and identify elements of the Christian life. Omit the special gifts (12:6-8). After you have made your list, circle areas of lifestyle in which you would like to grow and list them here.

In this session we have studied a deep book. Yet the Letter to the Romans has led the uneducated as well as the educated to grace and peace in Christ. How do you account for that?

Write in your own words what you think it means to be justified by faith. (Look again at Romans 3:21-26, NRSV.)

IF YOU WANT TO KNOW MORE

Study the life of Martin Luther or John Wesley to see how the Letter to the Romans turned their lives around, giving a basis for their experience of grace and peace. Suggested biographies are *Here I Stand: A Life of Martin Luther,* by Roland Bainton (Abingdon Press), and *The Radical Wesley*, by Howard A. Snyder (InterVarsity Press, 1984; out of print. Check the public library or search online).

Paul's Letters

Paul's letters generally include the same elements in a similar sequence. Compare some of his letters and make notes below about the similarities and differences you find in style and content. Look at these letters in particular: Romans, First and Second Corinthians, Galatians, Philippians, First Thessalonians, and Philemon.

Address and Greeting

What is the pattern of Paul's address and greeting?

Thanksgiving or Prayer

What does Paul thank God for?

Content of the Letter

What point is Paul making, and what is to result?

Greetings to Others and Blessing

What is the nature of Paul's greetings and blessing?

"Pursue love, and use your ambition to try to get spiritual gifts." —1 Corinthians 14:1

8 Sound Teaching for Faithful Living

OUR HUMAN CONDITION

We hate to leave the lifestyles of the secular world. They have a certain corrupt familiarity. But if we convert to the faith and fellowship of Christ, we discover that people, including ourselves, are still argumentative, divisive, self-centered. The church is not as perfect as we thought it would be.

ASSIGNMENT

Paul's Corinthian letters are not so much concerned with theology and doctrine as with the affairs of the church. Watch for insights into the life of the early church and for Paul's suggestions for solving its problems, many of which continue to trouble the church today.

Pray daily before study:

"Examine me, LORD; put me to the test!
    Purify my mind and my heart.
Because your faithful love is right in front
        of me—
    I walk in your truth!" (Psalm 26:2-3).

Prayer concerns for the week:

Day 1 **Read 1 Corinthians 1–5** (fellow workers for God, sexual immorality).

Day 2 **Read 1 Corinthians 6–10** (problems in the church at Corinth).

Day 3 **Read 1 Corinthians 11–15** (various gifts but one Spirit, love is the greatest gift, the Resurrection).

Day 4 **Read 1 Timothy 1–4** (supervising and leading in God's household).

Day 5 **Read 1 Timothy 5–6** (Christian conduct)**; Titus 1–3** (instructions on being godly).

Day 6 **Read "The Bible Teaching" and the "Marks of Discipleship" and answer the questions.**

Day 7 **Rest, pray, and attend class.**

THE BIBLE TEACHING

Scholars say Paul wrote several letters to the Corinthian church, some of which have been combined into First and Second Corinthians. The Corinthians also wrote to Paul (1 Corinthians 7:1). Paul loved this church. He was its spiritual father; he visited it, sent messengers to it, asked its congregation for offerings for the poor in Jerusalem. He wrote these letters because he could not go himself. The letters are especially precious to us because they are graphic, concrete, specific. They chastise and encourage. They contain guidance a father wanted to give his spiritual children.

Keep in mind what Corinth was like. We have said it was a sea town. Rather than sail all the way around the coast, many ship owners preferred to move their small sailing ships on rollers across the narrow isthmus. Other ships stopped for trade and supplies. Not a sophisticated city like Athens, not a power city like Rome, not a holy city like Jerusalem, Corinth was a center of commerce for the eastern Mediterranean.

Everybody passed through—slaves from all over the empire, Roman soldiers, Greeks, Persians, Syrians. In Corinth people practiced every conceivable vice. Jews in Corinth were definitely strangers in a strange land. The markets sold meat that had been offered to idols in pagan temples. Prostitutes walked the streets and served in the temples. Every day, including Sabbath, was hurly-burly business in the marketplace.

The Corinthian congregation contained a few converted Jews, a few God-fearers (persons who believed in the Jewish God without becoming Jews), but mostly Gentiles who had been converted to Christ from paganism. These Gentile converts had not been steeped in the law of Moses concerning sexual morality, Sabbath worship, tithing, food laws, hospitality, marriage within the religion, sobriety, devotion to Torah, or respect for the authority of the elders.

Unity

Given a dog-eat-dog economy, a mixed social scene with constant competition, it is no wonder there was bickering. Paul pleaded, "Don't be divided into rival groups" (1 Corinthians 1:10), but they did. Some persons were boasting that they had been converted by Paul. Others were proud they had been converted under Apollos. Some claimed that they adhered strictly to Peter's teachings. A few announced pompously that they were above all that: They belonged to Jesus. Paul was angry: Was Paul crucified for you? or Apollos? No, Jesus Christ is not divided (1:13).

Some claimed that they were wise in the ways of Christianity, perhaps because they were charter members, or because they knew the Hebrew Scriptures, or because they had more education. Others, influenced by gnosticism that taught a secret, saving "knowledge," said they knew secrets that no one else knew.

Paul used many images of unity—the human body in 1 Corinthians 12, a building in 1 Corinthians 3. The task is to fit together, complement one another, be humble, and build up the body.

Sex

You can imagine the problems this group would have had with sexual conduct. Paul had promised the apostles in the Jerusalem Council that he would not allow immorality among the Gentile converts.

Study 1 Corinthians 5–7 and make note of Paul's comment on the following problems:

- a man sleeping with his father's wife (stepmother)
- sexual activity with prostitutes
- adultery and sexual perversion
- marriage
- sexual relations within marriage
- where marriage already exists with an unbeliever
- where a marriage is contemplated with an unbeliever
- the single life like Paul's
- if a man was already circumcised
- if a man was not circumcised
- marriage after the death of a spouse

Remember that in these matters Paul wanted nothing to stand in the way of zeal for the gospel. He also was influenced by his belief that Christ was coming soon. With regard to Paul's commitment to the single life, remember Jesus' teaching in Matthew 19:10-12. Notice too that Paul was cautious when offering pastoral advice on whether to marry: "I don't have a command from the Lord . . . , but I'll give my opinion as someone you can trust" (1 Corinthians 7:25). He concludes by saying, "I think that I have God's Spirit too" (7:40).

Why his emphasis on singleness? Because of his zeal for the gospel. Family life takes time and energy, and Paul had turned his total energy toward winning men and women to Christ. He wanted others to do the same.

Women

People misread Paul because they fail to understand his society. In ancient Near Eastern society women were either quiet in the back rooms while the men talked or were loose women of the streets. Suddenly, in the church, a revolution was occurring. Men and women were together in prayer, in testimony, in witness and work. Priscilla instructed Apollos in the ways of the Holy Spirit. Some women, ecstatic over their newly found freedom, let their hair down like women of the streets. Some, uninformed in the Scriptures, were like dry sponges, eager to soak it all up. They were continually asking questions, shattering social decorum, and aggravating the congregations. (Aren't we all similarly affected by newly found freedom?) Paul admonished the women to be quiet, to ask their questions of their husbands when they got home. Women were less constrained in their new world of acceptance and liberty. Order, wrote Paul—order, decorum, decency, and mutual respect between wives and husbands.

The miracle, the social revolution, was like the Pentecost gathering in the upper room. Men and women were together in Christian fellowship. Something new under the sun!

Food

Those to whom Paul wrote were freed from Jewish food laws (except they did not eat blood), but a religious problem existed regarding animals offered in pagan sacrifice (1 Corinthians 8). These new Christians did not offer sacrifices in the temples of Aphrodite or Zeus, of course. Nor did they go to celebrations where the meat was eaten as an act of worship. But much of the meat that had been sacrificed to idols was sold in meat markets. Should they eat that meat? Paul quotes the newly free people who said, "We know that a false god isn't anything in this world" (8:4). True, so meat is meat—except to some who only recently had been idol worshipers and who had a tender conscience on this matter. If they ate the meat that had been sacrificed to idols, they were afraid it would mean they were still worshiping Zeus or Aphrodite. What to do?

Paul said the issue is love. If you destroy someone else by your new freedom, you are not building up the church. "If food causes the downfall of my brother or sister, I won't eat meat again [that has once been dedicated in idol worship], or else I may cause my brother or sister to fall" (8:13).

Tongues

In every great revival of Christian faith, the Holy Spirit has poured forth. People have spoken in prayer language, *glossolalia,* unknown tongues. This experience is not mentioned in Matthew, Luke, or John, but it occurred in the Corinthian church. Paul even declared that he spoke in tongues. But the issue is love. The overriding concern is what builds up the church. Read carefully 1 Corinthians 12–14 as a unit, for the love chapter, 1 Corinthians 13, is set in the middle specifically to deal with speaking in tongues. The climax is really 14:1: "Pursue love."

Paul spoke in tongues, but he did not want his doing so to bring confusion in the church or to keep people from understanding the gospel.

But will it benefit the church? "In the church I'd rather speak five words in my right mind, than speak thousands of words in a tongue so that I can teach others" (14:19). So no one is put down, order and love in the church are restored, and the priority is rightly placed on helping newcomers find the truth of Christ.

Life After Death

Some people were saying there is no resurrection. Others were wondering how it would happen, what kind of bodies they would have. Paul's point is this: Without the resurrection there is no gospel. If there is no gospel, we are still dead in our sins, still Adam and Eve wandering in disobedience somewhere outside Eden (1 Corinthians 15:12-19).

The issue for Paul cut to the center of the gospel: Quit preaching the forgiveness of sins if Christ was destroyed. Quit offering hope for a new life if Jesus is dead. Quit believing in eternal joy with God if Jesus was martyred and sent to sleep forever in the mists of Sheol. Paul proclaims that Jesus not only bled and died for sinners, he also rose again in victory and power. His offering of forgiveness carries divine authority. And of ultimate significance to us, his resurrection is the breakthrough, the pioneer work that leads the way. The same power that raised Jesus will raise us from the dead. If Christ is alive, as we believe, we too shall live in new appropriate bodies with our Savior. Not only has sin been defeated; so has death. We don't need to be afraid anymore.

Timothy and Titus

Three short books, First and Second Timothy and Titus, are called the Pastoral Letters. They are more like manuals for Christian conduct and church administration than they are like personal letters. Priests and pastors, bishops, elders, and deacons listen carefully to the letters' instructions to Timothy.

Timothy's father was Greek (Acts 16:1), and his mother was a Jewish Christian. So, two streams of culture converged in him. Timothy was like a son to bachelor Paul, a faithful and trusted young colleague. His character was impeccable; he was conscientious almost to a fault. Paul commissioned Timothy as emissary to fledgling churches in Thessalonica and Corinth. The two men traveled together to Jerusalem and finally to Rome. At some point, Timothy shared Paul's imprisonment (Hebrews 13:23).

Pastoral Counsel to Timothy

Several points are made in the advice to Timothy.

1. **Help people adhere to the central doctrines of the faith; concentrate on the essentials.** Always in religious circles, some people want to argue, spin endless theological webs, talk about conflicting church histories or denominational doctrine. They end up in conflict and waste valuable time. (Keep in mind that what is being rejected is not knowledge or philosophy as we know it but rather the "superior, secret" knowledge of gnosticism.) Seriously searching for sound teachings is vastly different from irresponsibly debating ideas without any intention of personal commitment. In one case the Word becomes flesh; in the other case the Word becomes words.

2. **Teach diligently.** Teaching sound doctrine to growing Christians is a difficult and awesome responsibility. The Letter of James declares, "My brothers and sisters, not many of you should become teachers, because we know that we teachers will be judged more strictly" (James 3:1).

That is true, of course, because the teacher teaches and shapes the minds and the lives of the learners. Yet Timothy is urged to teach with diligence. "Hold on to the pattern of sound teaching that you heard from me. . . . Protect this good thing that has been placed in your trust through the Holy Spirit who lives in us" (2 Timothy 1:13-14).

To Paul and Timothy, teaching was more than "head knowledge." It meant making disciples, training people in the Christian walk. Biblical knowledge and the understanding of the scriptural meaning were essential. Today with the New Testament added to the Hebrew Scriptures, these words of Second Timothy are even more true: "Every scripture is inspired by God and is useful for teaching, for showing mistakes, for correcting, and for training character, so that the person who belongs to God can be equipped to do everything that is good" (3:16-17).

While it is true that not everyone should be a teacher, it is also true that the need for teachers is overwhelming. Already in the early church, the task was too great for the apostles. Just as Moses needed help in supervising the Israelites in the wilderness, so pastors and priests in a crowded world cannot carry on the teaching ministry without help from disciplined, trained lay teachers.

But you say, teaching is tough. Absolutely! Look again at the expectations laid on Timothy. He was expected to have the discipline of a soldier, the dedication of an athlete, the willingness of a farmer to work hard (2:1-7).

3. **Respect spiritual authority and leadership.** We are to learn and to teach respect for certain kinds of authority. We give respect and authority to bishops (literally "overseers," sometimes translated "presbyter" or "elder") and other church leaders. We expect spiritual leaders to care for their families, be sober, not hungry for money, apt teachers. They should be mature Christians rather than new converts who might become conceited (1 Timothy 3:1-7).

4. **Teach the church to care for the needy.** With normal sickness and death magnified by persecution and martyrdom, many widows existed with little hope of livelihood. The task was heavy for the early church. So every family was expected to take care of its own, for "If someone doesn't provide for their own family, and especially for a member of their household, they have denied the faith. They are worse than those who have no faith" (1 Timothy 5:8).

Also, young widows were instructed to remarry if possible lest "they learn to be lazy by going from house to house" (5:13). Keep in mind that opportunities for employment for women were almost nonexistent. Prostitution and slavery were the most likely options. But real widows, women over sixty, without family, were the responsibility of the church. The miracle of love in the congregation was to care for these women as long as they lived.

5. **Be careful with money.** Money can do much good and much harm. The law of Moses forbade stealing and covetousness.

Amos warned those who accumulated property at the expense of the poor. Jesus taught more about money than he did about prayer. He warned against anxiety over what we would eat and wear. "It's easier for a camel to squeeze through the eye of a needle than for a rich person to enter God's kingdom" (Matthew 19:24).

Timothy warns that disciples will be led astray by desire for money. "*The love of money* is the root of all kinds of evil. Some have wandered away from the faith and have impaled themselves with a lot of pain because they made money their goal" (1 Timothy 6:10, italics added).

Think carefully about what you read in the Bible. How can we avoid "love of money"?

Conclusion: The wisdom of the older has been imparted to the younger. Youth is no handicap. "Don't let anyone look down on you because you are young. Instead, set an example for the believers through your speech, behavior, love, faith, and by being sexually pure" (1 Timothy 4:12). Old age must pass the responsibilities of leadership to the young. Paul, in a final burst of inspiration, passed the torch to his spiritual son and disciple: "You must keep control of yourself in all circumstances. Endure suffering, do the work of a preacher of the good news, and carry out your service fully. I'm already being poured out like a sacrifice to God, and the time of my death is near. I have fought the good fight, finished the race, and kept the faith" (2 Timothy 4:5-7).

Wouldn't it be wonderful if every Christian believer could say those words at the close of life!

MARKS OF DISCIPLESHIP

The Pastoral Letters establish the standard: sound teaching of the central doctrines of the faith. Disciples seek such teaching from trained and faithful leaders.

Generally, in our churches we have not emphasized placing ourselves under spiritual authority. We respect individual conscience and place our ultimate authority in Jesus Christ.

What kind and amount of authority and respect should we give our church leaders?

Mark of Discipleship
Disciples seek sound teaching from faithful leaders and live in love.

Right now in your life, what do you do to place yourself under sound teaching from faithful leaders?

Paul pleaded for unity and love, especially in the church. What are specific ways you are growing in your ability to bring unity and love in the way you live?

Discipleship is costly. Starting with what you know about the real world—how anxiety over money can destroy families, lead the rich astray, immobilize the poor—write some guidelines for your own attitude toward money that will help you be obedient to Jesus Christ; provide for your family; increase your usefulness in the Kingdom; and protect you from greed, covetousness, stealing, and anxiety.

The Holy Spirit gives many gifts. Part of living in love is to use your spiritual gifts. In a few weeks, you will be prayerfully seeking the group's counsel about what your distinctive gifts are. Looking especially at 1 Corinthians 12, what are your thoughts at this point about your gifts?

In Session 12, you will complete a spiritual gifts inventory. If you would like to get a head start, go to *adultbiblestudies.com/ fasttrack*.

IF YOU WANT TO KNOW MORE

No city is more fascinating than ancient Corinth. No church more exasperating or with more exciting possibilities. Do some research on Corinth and report to the group.

Look up information on Titus and prepare to report briefly.

"Christ has set us free for freedom. Therefore, stand firm and don't submit to the bondage of slavery again."

—Galatians 5:1

9 The Son Shall Set Us Free

OUR HUMAN CONDITION

I don't know if I'm free. There are so many rules. Sometimes I do my own thing, acting as if there were no moral restraints. But other times I try to be "religious" and follow the rules taught to me by my family or my church. When I try to follow all the rules, I fail and feel guilty. When I have some success, I feel religious; but I'm not very happy.

ASSIGNMENT

As you read, sense the emotion that permeates Galatians. Paul is defending his message and ministry. Look particularly for his defense of his apostleship in 1:6–2:21, his defense of his gospel in 3:1–4:31, and his defense of his moral standards in 5:1–6:10.

Be alert to words that are keys to Paul's thought: *justification* (NRSV), *righteousness, faith, believing, promise, freedom, Spirit*. Keep in mind that the basic question of Galatians for modern readers is the question of relationship. How do people relate to God?

Pray daily before study:

"Have mercy on me, God,
    according to your faithful love!
Wipe away my wrongdoings
    according to your great compassion!
Wash me completely clean of my guilt;
    purify me from my sin!" (Psalm 51:1-2).

Prayer concerns for the week:

Day 1   **Read Galatians 1** (threat of a different gospel).

Day 2   **Read Galatians 2** (Paul's rebuke of Cephas).

Day 3   **Read Galatians 3–4** (faith superior to the law, purpose of the law).

Day 4   **Read Galatians 5** (Christian freedom).

Day 5   **Read Galatians 6** (the law of Christ).

Day 6   **Read "The Bible Teaching" and the "Marks of Discipleship" and answer the questions.**

Day 7   **Rest, pray, and attend class.**

THE BIBLE TEACHING

Galatians is a pivotal letter because it sets out the fundamental difference between living by the Law and living by faith. At issue is this question: Since Jesus was a Jew and revered and quoted the Hebrew Scriptures, and since Jesus was the Messiah, must Gentiles become Jews before they can become Christians?

Galatians has two powerful meanings for us. First, without Paul's teachings in Galatians the Christian church either might have remained a Jewish sect, holding on to Christ and Jewish law at the same time, or it might have spun off into a new religion without roots in Judaism and the Hebrew Scriptures. It did neither.

Second, Galatians helps us become free from a religion of rules without becoming morally reckless. We avoid being "legalistic" on one hand or "libertine" on the other.

Galatia was a region in Asia Minor, not a city. Several congregations were scattered there. Paul had founded some of them. Now he learned that some Jewish and Gentile Christians had come into these churches and were spreading false and dangerous doctrines. They questioned Paul's authority, accusing him of not being Jewish enough, not being a true apostle, and perhaps demeaning him for his "weakness." Besides that, Paul wasn't there to defend himself. The issues were so crucial that Paul wrote in frustration and anger, "If anyone preaches something different from what you received [and some were], they should be under a curse!" (Galatians 1:9). Again, "I wish that the ones who are upsetting you would castrate themselves!" (5:12). His words were harsh, but Paul was dealing with spiritual life-and-death matters.

Who were these troublemakers? They may have been Judaizers, the same Jewish Aramaic-speaking Christians who gave Paul so much trouble back in Antioch over the decision by Greek-speaking Jewish Christians to convert Gentiles without requiring circumcision. They may have been Gentiles who had converted to Judaism, been circumcised, and later converted to Christianity. In any event, they discredited Paul's emphasis on total salvation through the work of Jesus Christ.

They kept suggesting that, yes, faith in Christ was important, but other things were also important: circumcision; certain Jewish food laws; special Jewish holy days; Jewish attitudes toward ethnic origin, social status, or gender.

These Gentile or Jewish Christians may have been influenced by the gnostics who believed there were higher forms of knowledge, higher levels of righteousness. If such belief was combined with Jewish ritual and practice, persons could gain salvation by their achievements.

Paul blasted these ideas because they resembled the idea of earned redemption. He, better than they, knew the full meaning of the Law. They were playing with it; he had taken it absolutely seriously. He had been Pharisee of the Pharisees, trying with total life commitment to keep every aspect of the Law. Why? Because if you are going to be saved by the Law, you have to keep it all, not just selected parts.

Circumcision for Paul was not just a ritual. It was a sign of placing oneself under Jewish law. Are you going to follow Jewish law literally? Are you going to count your steps on the Sabbath? Are you going to observe every one of the Jewish holy days as prescribed in Leviticus? Are you going to eat certain foods and not eat others? Or are you going to interpret the Law more flexibly? Are you willing to heal the sick on the Sabbath? Are you willing to eat with non-Jews (including the Lord's Supper, because the Lord's Supper and the church supper were not yet separated)? Are you willing to eat in their homes? Will you work side by side with women? with Gentiles?

You who want to say that belonging to Christ Jesus is not enough, that there are other things you must do, where will you stop? Is God's saving work in Jesus Christ not enough? Does the righteousness Christ Jesus gives satisfy only ninety percent of your needs?

Either you are saved by God through the cross of Jesus Christ or you are not, declared Paul. You can't have it halfway or both ways.

Paul reminded his readers that even Peter and Barnabas had wavered. They had seen with their own eyes uncircumcised Gentiles converted, forgiven, filled with the Holy Spirit, motivated by love of Jesus and neighbor. Yet, when criticized by conservative Jews for eating with Gentiles, they drew back. Paul had confronted Peter face-to-face. Either they (Peter and Barnabas) were saved by grace or not. Either they were one in Christ or not. Paul understood clearly. They could not have it both ways (Galatians 2).

Now Paul had to deal with related issues: Why then did we have the law of Moses in the first place? To show what wrongdoing is and to restrain us from sin. The Law, Paul wrote, took care of us the way a legal guardian takes care of a minor who is not yet ready to assume full responsibilities. But now, in Jesus Christ, we've come of age; we've been fully adopted. We live not by rules but in relationship (3:21–4:7).

Historical Observations

Most people play with the law, and then only parts of it, obeying it when it pleases them. When someone comes along who takes the law seriously or misunderstands the function of the law, it leads to imprisonment of the soul.

Martin Luther, trying to please God, became a monk, then a Roman Catholic priest, then a scholar and ascetic—fasting, studying the Bible, confessing daily, whipping himself to the point of exhaustion, finally going to Rome and kissing the steps of Saint Peter's Church. Were not these acts works of righteousness? Did they not bring saving grace? No, for Luther, they were imprisoning. When his salvation came, he knew that he was saved by the grace of God alone. As he was reading Romans, he wrote beside 1:17

the Latin words *sola fide* ("faith alone"). All the weight of the law fell off his shoulders; and he felt he was accepted, forgiven, and loved as a child of God. No strings attached.

John Wesley walked a similar path. Child of a preacher, honor student, thrifty, sexually pure, respectful of mother and father. He visited the prisons, fasted, prayed, studied Scripture in Greek and Hebrew, became an Anglican priest and then a missionary to Georgia.

But at Aldersgate he felt the burden of keeping the law fall away. He said that he felt his heart strangely warmed. He felt he did trust in Christ alone for salvation. He felt the personal assurance that Christ had taken away his sins and had saved him from the law of sin and death.

The Freedom Lifestyle

Now the issue becomes this: What do believers do with their freedom? "You were called to freedom, brothers and sisters; only don't let this freedom be an opportunity to indulge your selfish impulses, but serve each other through love" (Galatians 5:13).

Believers are not only saved by Christ; they are called to live in Christ. The new life is the life of love, for "all the Law has been fulfilled in a single statement, '*Love your neighbor as yourself*'" (5:14). The whole purpose of the Law was to cause the people of God to love God and neighbor. Now in Christ, people not only do fulfill the Law but rejoice in doing so.

The new creation lives above the law; that is, as Jesus suggested, a life more righteous than that of those who lived by the Law. To Paul, flesh did not mean physical passion; rather, flesh referred to the old Adam, the self-centered, unconverted person of the world. The way of self-centeredness is plain: "The actions that are produced by selfish motives are obvious, since they include sexual immorality, moral corruption, doing whatever feels good, idolatry, drug use and casting spells, hate, fighting, obsession, losing your temper, competitive opposition, conflict, selfishness, group rivalry, jealousy, drunkenness, partying, and other things like that" (5:19-21).

But when believers are living in the Spirit, in Christ, they want to please God—not as a burden, but because they love God. They live in God. They want to live lives better than the Law.

A son or a daughter can live grudgingly according to household rules. But a loving son or daughter can move beyond that into an acceptance, a fellowship, a spiritual unity. "The fruit of the Spirit," which is in those who live in Christ's Spirit, "is love, joy, peace, patience, kindness, goodness, faithfulness, gentleness, and self-control. There is no law against things like this" (5:22-23).

An old legend tells of people who came wanting to buy the fruit of the Spirit. They were told, "We don't sell the fruit; we sell the seeds." Indeed, these traits of the holy life are not forced, not strived for, certainly not bought. Rather, they grow out of the believer's heart. They grow out of the indwelling presence of Jesus, the promised Holy Spirit.

Paul wants us to be free—free to love, free to embrace the very intent of the Law in joyous obedience, free to live in the harmony God intended from the beginning of Creation. "If we live by the Spirit, let's follow the Spirit" (5:25). That means we will "carry each other's burdens" (6:2). That means, "So then, let's work for the good of all whenever we have an opportunity, and especially for those in the household of faith" (6:10).

We, like Paul, freed from the Law's domination, are able to serve with a joyous heart. Freedom and love fill us; the old rules no longer hold us. We move from thinking of right living as a precondition of salvation to understanding faith itself as the way to true holiness.

Legalism and Libertinism

Christianity has often developed legalisms—moralisms that believers were supposed to accept in addition to the grace of God in Christ. Religious leaders often seem afraid to trust believers with spiritual freedom. What were some of these legalisms? Sometimes it was going to church on Wednesdays and Sundays, or refraining from playing games on the Lord's day. Sometimes it was wearing dark clothes, carrying a Bible, not going to movies, shunning jewelry or dancing. Sometimes it meant staying in the rural community, marrying within a particular denomination, or not shaving one's beard. Sometimes it was not raising questions about what the Bible says.

On the other hand, we might ask what makes these behaviors legalisms. Is one free from legalism by violating these restrictions?

As you contemplate present-day church life, what legalisms do you perceive that seem to be binding us up?

If we, as individuals or as a society, have come out of a period of legalism into a time of unrestrained freedom, what direction or guidance shall we follow for living and choosing?

The other danger is libertinism, that is, doing anything we please. The Danish theologian Søren Kierkegaard accused nineteenth-century Christians in Denmark of being careless and indifferent to the true Christian life. They used their baptism as an excuse to live like worldly people. Dietrich Bonhoeffer, a twentieth-century German pastor, termed such understanding of Christianity "cheap grace."

> "Cheap grace is the deadly enemy of our Church. We are fighting to-day for costly grace. . . .
> "Cheap grace means grace as a doctrine, a principle, a system. . . .
> "Cheap grace means the justification of sin without the justification of the sinner. . . .
> "Cheap grace is the preaching of forgiveness without requiring repentance, baptism without church discipline, Communion without confession, absolution without personal confession.
> "Cheap grace is grace without discipleship, grace without the cross, grace without Jesus Christ."*

* From Dietrich Bonhoeffer, *The Cost of Discipleship* (New York: The Macmillan Company, 1949), 35–36.

Martin Luther, coming out of legalism, embraced freedom. He put Galatians to his lips like a trumpet, someone wrote, and blew the reveille of the Reformation.

But Bonhoeffer, a modern Lutheran, was afraid of just the opposite—a freedom without discipline, without devotion, without divine direction.

How can we move to a new costly grace without external, imposed rules and religious laws?

MARKS OF DISCIPLESHIP

Disciples are people whose faith is nourished by hope, whose life is powered by love. Disciples are set free by Christ to love. Their newly found freedom does not cause them to do whatever they wish, but rather to live a loving and self-giving life, a lifestyle higher than any set of rules.

Start with the understanding of freedom as loving God and loving your neighbor as yourself. Think about dilemmas that cause you to ask the question, "Am I free or under rules?" What dilemmas are solved by this understanding of freedom?

Don't forget to take the spiritual gifts inventory located at *adultbiblestudies.com/fasttrack* for Session 12.

IF YOU WANT TO KNOW MORE

A book we will not have time to read is Paul's Letter to the Philippians. Written from prison in Rome, it nevertheless fairly bubbles with joy, with the kind of love Galatians speaks about pouring freely from the heart. Read Philippians. Look for the model of unity and harmony provided by Christ in Philippians 2:6-11.

Mark of Discipleship
Disciples experience and express freedom as loving God and loving neighbor.

"Also, let's hold on to the confession since we have a great high priest who passed through the heavens, who is Jesus, God's Son; because we don't have a high priest who can't sympathize with our weaknesses but instead one who was tempted in every way that we are, except without sin.

"Finally, let's draw near to the throne of favor with confidence so that we can receive mercy and find grace when we need help."　—Hebrews 4:14-16

10　Our Great High Priest

OUR HUMAN CONDITION

We cannot figure out a way to atone for our sins. Our faith grows weary and powerless. So we live lives of quiet desperation or turn to beating ourselves, wringing our hands, anesthetizing our spiritual pain with alcohol or other drugs, or developing neurotic symptoms.

ASSIGNMENT

From childhood we were taught, "Jesus Christ is the same yesterday, today, and forever" (Hebrews 13:8). As you read Hebrews, you will discover many verses, phrases, and ideas familiar to you from their frequent use in the sermons, hymns, and rituals of the church. Scattered throughout the book you will find clues to its purpose: In the face of persecution and suffering, a kind of apathy or weariness in the faith was taking over. The writer calls readers to steadiness, patience, and endurance.

Pray daily before study:

"You are LORD God All-Powerful!
　No one is as loving
　and faithful as you are"
　　　　(Psalm 89:8, CEV).

Prayer concerns for the week:

Day 1 **Read Hebrews 1–3** (superiority of Christ).

Day 4 **Read Hebrews 9–10** (earthly sanctuary, mediator of a new covenant).

Day 2 **Read Hebrews 4–6** (priesthood of Christ).

Day 5 **Read Hebrews 11–13** (nature of faith, meaning of discipline, sacrifices pleasing to God).

Day 3 **Read Hebrews 7–8** (levitical priesthood imperfect).

Day 6 **Read "The Bible Teaching" and the "Marks of Discipleship" and answer the questions.**

Day 7 **Rest, pray, and attend class.**

THE BIBLE TEACHING

Hebrews is a mystery book to those who do not know Leviticus. Today the animal sacrifices and blood offerings commanded in Leviticus seem bizarre, even abhorrent, ancient rituals.

But are we so wise, we moderns? Where will we go to get rid of our guilt? What is the cure for our anxious consciences? What will take away our sin?

Some Christians were giving up, falling away. Why? Persecution. Fading faith. Pressure on some from the Jewish community. Hebrews was written to say that Christians must stand fast as did the faithful men and women of old. It declares that Jesus is greater than the prophets, greater than the angels, greater than Moses. Hebrews proclaims that the once-and-for-all sacrifice of Jesus Christ ushers Christians into a clean conscience and an eternal salvation.

To understand Hebrews, we need to know these terms:

Purification for sins (1:3, NRSV): Purification by water, blood, and sacrifice was necessary to the Jews to be clean from moral, physical, and ritualistic impurity.

Sanctify (2:11, NRSV): to make holy—to set apart for God's service; to make fit for God's presence through cleansing from sin.

Sacrifice of atonement (2:17, NRSV): wiping out the sin, doing away with what offends.

High priest (4:14, NRSV): the sanctuary official who entered the Holy of Holies on the annual Day of Atonement to sprinkle blood on the mercy seat (Exodus 25:17-22; Leviticus 16:14-16).

Melchizedek (Hebrews 5:6, NRSV): means "king of righteousness," blessed Abraham (Genesis 14:17-20), came to be regarded as the ideal priest-king who foreshadowed the Davidic king and later the Messiah (Psalm 110).

Levitical priesthood (Hebrews 7:11, NRSV): descendants of Levi who performed the rituals in the sanctuary. The priesthood was inherited since the Levites did not receive land.

New covenant (8:8, NRSV): term originating with Jeremiah (Jeremiah 31:31), a new arrangement between God and God's people in which God's law would be written on the people's hearts.

Holy of Holies (Hebrews 9:3, NRSV): The Tabernacle, and later the Temple, was divided into three parts: an open-air court; the Holy Place; and behind a curtain, the Holy of Holies or "the place where God speaks." The Holy of Holies (Most Holy Place) contained the ark of the covenant. Theologically, the belief emerged that God resided permanently in the Holy of Holies (1 Kings 8:12-13).

Ark of the covenant (Hebrews 9:4, NRSV): a wooden chest that served as a portable shrine, overlaid with gold, contained the two tablets of the Law. Hebrews reflects later Jewish tradition that it also contained manna and Aaron's miraculous rod.

Atonement

Our needs are different from the needs of those to whom Hebrews was addressed, and yet they are the same. They needed to realize that animal sacrifices were no longer necessary. We too face the need for cleansing, for inner purification and peace. But we find it difficult to grasp that a sacrifice is necessary, that a sacrifice is available to us, and that a sacrifice can be appropriated into our spiritual lives.

In deep, closely reasoned argument, Hebrews shows the way by reminding us who Jesus is. He is the Son of God; he is "the imprint of God's being" (Hebrews 1:3). No angel would be adequate to meet our needs because the angel does not touch our humanity. No prophet of old could fulfill the complete ministry because the prophet does not transcend the human. Neither Moses nor the Law of the first covenant could save us, for Moses was a servant; Jesus was the Son. Hebrews proclaims that Jesus "shared the same things" (2:14) as all of us. He was human as we are human.

Anselm, a twelfth-century theologian, wrote that Jesus had to be fully human in order to reach us and had to be fully God in order to save us. He echoed Hebrews.

Now comes the overwhelming comparison. The old covenant was ratified by blood, the blood of animals sacrificed to God. The new covenant was also confirmed by blood, the blood of Jesus Christ. No other sacrifice will ever be needed.

Covenant always means a compact entailing God's loving initiative and humankind's response in faithfulness. As you recall God's covenant with Abraham (Genesis 15; 17:1-22), confirmed in the law of Moses, list some essential promises of God and responses by the people in that covenant. Here are some references to help: Exodus 19:1-6; 24:1-8, 12, 15-18; 25:8, 10, 16-17, 21-22; 28:1-4; 29:1-9; 30:1-10; 31:12-18.

The prophets recognized the weakness of formal religion and the dangers of going through external motions without internal, spiritual, and moral reality. Look up again Amos 5:21-24 and Isaiah 1:12-17. Now read Jeremiah 31:31-34.

Notice that Hebrews quotes Jeremiah to show that the first covenant had become faulty and obsolete (Hebrews 8:6-13).

Hebrews spotlights the blood sacrifice, which was at the heart of the first covenant. If a religion is going to have high moral expectations and important prescribed duties, that religion must have a way to remove guilt, for, as Paul wrote to the Romans, "all have sinned and fall short of God's glory" (Romans 3:23). Hebrews argues against going back to the old animal sacrifice when God has initiated a cleansing new covenant through the eternal Son and his sacrifice. Study Hebrews to see the careful parallels between the first covenant and the new covenant. Notice that it is the same God who acted in both covenants.

What were the sacrifices offered for sin? (Don't forget the scapegoat.) Look at Leviticus 16.

Who offered the sacrifices in the first covenant?

Where did they receive their authority?

Why do you think the sacrifices continued daily in the Temple in Jesus' day?

What was the sacrifice Jesus offered?

Who was this Jesus who offered the sacrifice in the new covenant?

Where did he receive his authority?

Notice that Jesus was not a levitical priest but a descendant of the tribe of Judah. That is where the strange reference to Melchizedek comes in—no genealogy, no birth, no death, no reference to Aaron or the Levites. In fact, this strange, mysterious priest-king is greater than Abraham or Levi. His order of priesthood is directly from God, not inherited or transmitted.

The former priests were "numerous" (Hebrews 7:23); Jesus stands alone. They died, so new ones had to be chosen. Jesus "holds the office of priest permanently" (7:24).

Although the animals were to be without spot or blemish, they had to be offered by imperfect priests over and over. In Jesus, the offering was without sin, and the offerer was without sin. It was a perfect sacrifice, done once and for all (7:27; 10:11-14).

Jesus was no martyr, struck down by political intrigue. He was God in human person, offering a perfect gift of love and life's blood sacrifice for the sins of the whole world.

The word *atonement* means to remove the barrier of sin and guilt separating people and God. Jesus the mediator bridges the separation. He brings peace between the two. Atonement means "at-one-ment," the Holy God at one with us.

Hebrews points to the power of the divine sacrifice to cleanse our hearts. Remember that repentance was always necessary for the sacrifice to be effective. Repentance does not mean simply saying, "I'm sorry"; it means a turning away from sin and a turning toward God, a turning over of life's purpose to the loving will of God.

Atonement makes possible a new creature, clean and at peace with God. To experience "the blood" is to experience the forgiveness or grace of God. The Letter to the Hebrews insists, "There is no forgiveness without blood being shed" (9:22). Blood is the ultimate sacrifice. In the Bible "blood" and "life" were the same. The ancients thought that life was in the blood. As the blood drained out, the life drained out. To give one's blood is to give one's life.

"Hold On"

Because Hebrews is concerned about those who might fall away from this great salvation, the book reminds us to "hold on" and to "consider each other carefully for the purpose of sparking love and good deeds. Don't stop meeting together with other believers, which some people have gotten into the habit of doing. Instead, encourage each other" (Hebrews 10:23-25).

Some people, as they drift away from fellowship, from Holy Communion, from scriptural remembrances, and from mutual encouragement, forget the work of Christ on the cross and forget his intercessory pleas on their behalf.

Hebrews now becomes stern. If after receiving this great sacrifice, we drift away and "make the decision to sin," we face "a scary expectation of judgment" (10:26-27). "How much worse punishment [than a person violating the law of Moses] do you think is deserved by the person who walks all over God's Son, who acts as if the blood of the covenant that made us holy is just ordinary blood, and who insults the Spirit of grace? . . . It's scary to fall into the hands of the living God" (10:29-31).

Few passages in Scripture are as powerful and as inspiring as Hebrews 11–13. In an effort to encourage Christians to hold fast to their faith, the writer recalls witnesses "given approval for their faith" (11:39)—Abel, Enoch, Noah, Abraham, Sarah, Isaac, Jacob, Joseph, Moses, Rahab. They inspire us. Yet—and here the writer makes a fascinating point—their full salvation hinges on the way we live our lives. In spite of their great faith, they need us in order to be perfected.

We need them; they need us. "So then . . . let's throw off any extra baggage, get rid of the sin that trips us up, and fix our eyes on Jesus, faith's pioneer and perfecter" (12:1-2).

Hold on. "So strengthen your drooping hands and weak knees!" (12:12).

The Moral Imperative

"Keep loving each other like family. . . . Open up your homes to guests [as Abraham did in Genesis 18]. . . . Remember prisoners as if you were in prison with them. . . . Marriage must be honored in every respect, with no cheating on the relationship. . . . Your way of life should be free from the love of money," for "Jesus Christ is the same yesterday, today, and forever!" (Hebrews 13:1-5, 8).

MARKS OF DISCIPLESHIP

A sacrifice can be powerful. A mother scrubs floors so her daughter can go to college. An older brother offers a kidney transplant so his younger brother can live. A man or woman chooses a vocation like teaching or preaching or scientific research at considerable financial sacrifice. A pilot missionary is shot by a rebel soldier, making the final sacrifice for faith.

A sacrifice is measured by who is giving it, by whether it is voluntary, by how much the sacrifice costs, and by the cause in which the sacrifice is given.

A pastor sometimes has a person come into the study acknowledging a serious sin. The pastor may speak of forgiveness, but the person responds, "I guess it is true that God forgives people. But I don't know whether God can forgive me. Even if there was some sort of divine forgiveness, I don't think I could ever forgive myself."

If that person could listen to you, what would you say?

Describe an experience of mercy, an "amazing grace" in which you felt that your sins were forgiven and that you were cleansed and made right with God.

Mark of Discipleship
Disciples accept God's forgiveness.

Because even in a state of salvation we do things we ought not to do and do not do things we ought to do (Romans 7:19), we need continual forgiveness. Read 1 John 1:7-9. How do you receive day-by-day forgiveness?

Not only are we surrounded by a great cloud of biblical witnesses, but we also have some people in our lifetime cheering us on. List a few people across your life or right now who are pulling for you and encouraging you to be a faithful Christian.

If they are still alive, why not drop them a note, thanking them for their encouragement? Jot down some things you would want to say to them here.

Don't forget to take the spiritual gifts inventory located at *adultbiblestudies.com/fasttrack* for Session 12.

IF YOU WANT TO KNOW MORE

Read aloud Hebrews 11–13.

Sing or read the words of some hymns about atonement, for example, "Rock of Ages, Cleft for Me," "Jesus, Lover of My Soul," "Just as I Am, Without One Plea," "When I Survey the Wondrous Cross," "How Great Thou Art."

"Then he said to me, 'These words are trustworthy and true. The Lord, the God of the spirits of the prophets, sent his angel to show his servants what must soon take place.

"'Look! I'm coming soon. Favored is the one who keeps the words of the prophecy contained in this scroll.'"

—Revelation 22:6-7

11 We Never Lose Hope

OUR HUMAN CONDITION

Wars and rumors of wars continue. Prejudice, crime, disease, and drugs pervade the planet. Weeping and pain and death are constant. Justice eludes us. Where is the victory? Where is hope?

ASSIGNMENT

Do not get bogged down in detail. You are listening to an urgent sermon by an inspired preacher pleading for repentance. You are hearing an exile on the sun-baked island of Patmos, urging the faithful to remain steadfast. You are reading an ecstatic vision of end times that is more like poetry than prose. Savor the imagery; rejoice in the exuberant shouts of victory. Don't be squeamish: Christians were and are living and dying in a world of war, famine, persecution, exploitation, and violence. Those who suffer for their faith cling closely to John's Revelation.

Pray daily before study:

"Praise the LORD, all you nations!
   Worship him, all you peoples!
Because God's faithful love toward us
      is strong,
   the LORD's faithfulness lasts forever!
Praise the LORD!" (Psalm 117).

Prayer concerns for the week:

Day 1 **Read "The Bible Teaching" section, stopping before "The Message to Us" and the "Marks of Discipleship." Then read Revelation 1–3** (the letters to the seven churches).

Day 4 **Read Revelation 13–16** (beast with seven heads, a new song, seven bowls of wrath).

Day 2 **Read Revelation 4–7** (the Lamb, six seals).

Day 5 **Read Revelation 17–20** (doom of Babylon, bride of the Lamb, the Last Judgment).

Day 3 **Read Revelation 8–12** (seventh seal, angels with trumpets, the woman and the dragon).

Day 6 **Read Revelation 21–22, "The Message to Us," and the "Marks of Discipleship" and answer the questions.**

Day 7 **Rest, pray, and attend class.**

DISCIPLE FAST TRACK

THE BIBLE TEACHING

Nero lighted Rome by burning Christians on tar-soaked crosses in A.D. 64. Others were crucified or decapitated. Apparently, both Peter and Paul were martyred at that time in Rome. Tradition says that Peter was crucified upside down because he said he was not worthy to be crucified as Jesus was. Vespasian, Nero's successor, sent his son Titus to destroy Jerusalem in A.D. 70 in an effort to put down the Jews. When Domitian became Roman emperor in A.D. 81 and declared himself a god, the entire empire trembled. Domitian, a jealous, moody, unpredictable tyrant, cut down everyone he considered a threat. He executed his niece's husband on a charge of atheism, presumably for his refusing to consider Domitian a god. Coins found around the empire show his face and the words *Domitian Divine Caesar*. He demanded worship of himself as lord and god.

Domitian used selective terrorist tactics against the Christians during his reign (A.D. 81–96). A letter from Clement of Rome to the church at Corinth about A.D. 95 refers to "the sudden and repeated misfortunes and calamities which have befallen us."

A new temple for the cult of the emperor was built in Ephesus, putting additional pressure on the Christians of Asia. John, the author of Revelation, was exiled on Patmos, the penal island for political offenders, because of his loyalty to Christ (Revelation 1:9). A Christian named Antipas, a member of the church in Pergamum (a center of emperor worship), had been put to death for his fidelity to Jesus (2:13).

John says that some Christians in Smyrna will face death (2:10), and he prophesied that even more fierce persecution lay ahead for the church. Persecution did continue from time to time until the emperor Constantine saw a cross in the sky and became sympathetic to Christianity in A.D. 312. John wanted his revelation to give Christians encouragement to hold fast and remain faithful to the Lord. Take heart; the martyrs would be close to the altar of the Lord (6:9-11).

A Difficult Book

Most scholars today believe that a great Christian leader, highly respected and very well known in Asia and whose name was John, wrote his Revelation toward the end of this time of trouble, tension, and impending martyrdom (A.D. 81–96). A probable date for the writing would be A.D. 95/96. Scholars debate whether the author was John the apostle or another John.

The title of the book is "The Apocalypse," which means revelation. It has been translated "The Revelation to John" and has come to mean the revelation of end times. We were introduced to apocalyptic literature in Daniel. Prophecy in apocalyptic writings moves beyond preaching about soon-to-come events, as in Amos or Hosea, and enters into visions of last days or end times.

We know that we are going to have difficulty understanding the book. Everyone does, for several reasons.

First, apocalypses do not yield their messages easily to us because we are so far removed from the historical events, strange symbols, and ancient concepts. We must first ask what the book meant to its original readers. Like Daniel seeing visions of beasts (Daniel 7), like Ezekiel seeing the valley of the dry bones (Ezekiel 37), so John is describing his vision in symbolic language for his day. We are reading a spiritual vision of end times in ancient terms.

Second, as John said, he was caught up in the Spirit. An important gift of the Holy Spirit is the ability to prophesy, to proclaim the truths of God. John claimed to be standing in the role of prophet, caught up in the Spirit of God. "I was in the a Spirit-induced trance on the Lord's day" (Revelation 1:10). In a vision he ate a scroll (God's Word) as Ezekiel had done (10:10; Ezekiel 2:8–3:3). And he was told, "You must prophesy again" (Revelation 10:11).

A third reason the book is difficult is that it was intended to be. Ordinary words lacked the power to carry its message. So John used symbolic language from the Old Testament—reinterpreting the symbols and images for his day. To outsiders it was meaningless. But to insiders the message was clear. They understood the symbolic language:

- Babylon—really means Rome, the great city set on seven hills (18:2)
- the great beast like a leopard, bear, lion—the evil empires of Daniel, now rolled into one—the Roman Empire (13:1-2)
- the great whore—again, Rome
- the Lamb—Jesus
- the beast—the antichrist
- Sodom—Jerusalem (11:8; see Isaiah 1:9-10)
- the woman (Israel), the child (Jesus), and the dragon (Satan) (Revelation 12)
- the scarlet beast—the Roman Empire (17:3)
- "full of blasphemous names" (17:3; 13:1)—divine titles given to Roman emperors (17:9-11)
- Harmagedon (Armageddon)—hill of Megiddo in Palestine where important battles had been fought for thousands of years, symbolically the place of final victory (16:16)

In ancient numerology, numbers had meanings:

Number 1 stood for God, a holy number.
Number 3 stood for heaven and the Trinity.
Number 4 stood for earth, the four corners, four winds.
Number 6 is a human number, incomplete, evil.
Number 7 was considered perfect, complete, holy, divine because it was the combination of 3 (heaven) and 4 (earth). Seven churches, seven candlesticks, seven bowls (as in the Temple), seven trumpets. (We still say, "We're at sixes and sevens," meaning that evil and good do not mix or that we cannot decide between two choices.)

Number 13 has been an "unlucky" number for hundreds of years because it is the sum of six and seven.

Number 12 is very important in Revelation. Twelve tribes of Israel in the Old Testament and twelve apostles in the New Testament refer to the people of God. The twelve tribes provided gates into the holy city.

Number 24 is two times twelve, the twelve sons of Jacob (tribes) and the twelve apostles. Together they comprise the faithful Jews and Christians of the full covenant.

Twelve thousand times twelve is 144,000, a complete number, not to be taken literally, but to describe a "perfected people of God," the complete household of faith.

The number 666: How would you mention the emperor Domitian without getting your head cut off? You could write 666, which means evil, evil, evil, symbolizing Domitian—the greatest evil. The language was complex but necessary to communicate the message to those for whom it was intended.

The Message to the Christians in Asia

Briefly, remember these four points:

1. The churches are called to burn again with the passionate fire of evangelism and faithfulness: Shun food offered to idols, immorality, the libertine teachings of the Nicolaitans who said "anything goes." Avoid the Jews who are harassing the churches. Do not have an eye to money. Repent of lukewarm religion, and God will save you from falling away during times of stress.

2. John warns that trouble is coming. Be sure which side you are on. The four horsemen—conquest, war, famine, and death— are coming. Earthquakes and plagues (as in Egypt) are God's way of giving last-minute warnings, but many will not repent. Notice in Revelation 11:1-2 that the courtyard outside the Temple where foreign visitors or curious inquirers gathered will be trampled. You are either in or out, washed in the blood of Christ or doomed, wearing either the mark of the Lamb or the mark of the beast.

3. Rome will fall. "Fallen, fallen is Babylon the great!" (18:2). Right then it appeared that Rome was all-powerful; but remember, as Isaiah said, "The nations are like a drop in a bucket" (Isaiah 40:15). Stand firm. The day will soon come when the Roman Empire, awful whore, slayer of God's people, will be gone from the face of the earth.

4. Evil will be destroyed once and for all. Christ is married to his bride, his holy people (Revelation 19:7). Satan first will be bound (20:2) and then finally thrown into a lake of fire (20:10). Even death itself shall die (20:14), and God will bring a new heaven and a new earth (21:1).

The Message to Us

Read carefully Revelation 21–22. Notice that the God who will bring a new heaven and a new earth is the same God who created Adam and Eve, who called Abraham and Sarah, and who gave his only Son. "I am the Alpha and the Omega, the beginning and the end" (21:6). The one God of the universe will redeem the whole creation.

In one sense, redemption is complete. "All is done!" said the one who sits on the throne (21:6). But in another sense, God's mercy is still open, even in this last hour. To the repentant, God will still reach out. "To the thirsty I will freely give water from the life-giving spring" (21:6).

The faithful must hold on, living the Christlike life, for they are married to the bridegroom, the Lamb of God. "Those who emerge victorious will inherit these things. I will be their God and they will be my sons and daughters" (21:7). Do not sell out or betray the Lamb!

The holy city is symbolic in its size, its imagery, its gates, its light. What do you think each symbol means (21:10-27)? What meaning do the symbols have for you?

Watch carefully the closing of the book, beginning in 22:6. "Look! I'm coming soon" (22:7). There is still time to offer the gospel to others.

"Favored is the one who keeps the words of the prophecy contained in this scroll" (22:7). In Revelation 11, two witnesses prophesied, clothed in sackcloth. They appealed to people to repent. In the earthquake seven thousand were killed, but "the rest were afraid and gave glory to the God of heaven" (11:13).

A moment of possibility remains.

Where does it end? It ends in a garden, a garden of innocence like the garden of Eden before the Fall. No evil is permitted there, not even a snake, for the tempter is dead. The spiritual death has been overcome by the blood of the Lamb. Death has been slain. We stand beside a tree, in the intimacy of God. It is the tree of life, the "other" tree in the garden of Eden (Genesis 2:9). We are "naked" and not afraid.

Whereas Adam and Eve hid, lonely, guilt-ridden, afraid, hoping God would not find them, we will then live with God in the full light of day. The Bible begins with people hiding from God; it ends with people praying, "Come, Lord Jesus!" (Revelation 22:20).

We pray now for the coming, the soon coming, of the kingdom of God, which Jesus the Christ introduced and which he will one day fully complete. Meanwhile, we never lose hope, because the final victory belongs to Christ Jesus, our Savior and our Lord.

MARKS OF DISCIPLESHIP

The disciple must remain faithful even in the midst of persecution and suffering. No matter how bad the times, we hold on to our loyalty to Jesus Christ, knowing that the victory rests ultimately with God.

Most of us have suffered little for our faith, yet we are tempted to drift away. What do you think are the greatest temptations we face that would keep us from remaining faithful?

If you were to describe a "Babylon" today, what would it look like? Who or what would be its agents?

How is the vision of God's final victory helpful to you?

If time is short, and it certainly is for us as individuals, who are some people you should be praying for, witnessing to, right now? Name them.

NOTES

Mark of Discipleship
Disciples remain faithful to God in the midst of persecution and suffering.

Don't forget to take the spiritual gifts inventory located at *adultbiblestudies.com/fasttrack* for Session 12.

LOOK BACK ON YOUR JOURNEY AND REMEMBER

Record here the high points (and perhaps the low points) of your journey into and through the Bible—the insights, truths, and experiences you now treasure; the distances you traveled in time and faith; the friends you made and the companions you had along the way; and the view you now have of discipleship.

If you make my word your home you will indeed be my disciples.
—John 8:31, NJB

"We have many parts in one body, but the parts don't all have the same function. In the same way, though there are many of us, we are one body in Christ, and individually we belong to each other. We have different gifts that are consistent with God's grace that has been given to us."
—Romans 12:4-6

12 A People Set Apart

OUR HUMAN CONDITION

I don't like to be different. People ridicule others who seem strange and out of step with the crowd. And I surely don't want to be thought of as holy. But when I do try to serve God, sometimes I think that others can do so many things better than I can. I don't have any real talent or gifts that I can use in God's work.

ASSIGNMENT

As you read First Peter, think about what it means today, as a faithful disciple of Jesus Christ, to be part of "A People Set Apart." As you continue reading, you will see that part of being set apart is to discover and use your gifts for ministry. You will spend time considering your place of service in the body of Christ. Finally, you will remember that we are a covenant people, forgiven and freed by Christ.

Pray daily before study:

"Teach me, LORD, what you want me
    to do,
  and I will obey you faithfully;
  teach me to serve you with
    complete devotion"
      (Psalm 86:11, GNT).

Prayer concerns for the week:

Day 1 **Read 1 Peter 1–2; 3:8-9** (thanksgiving, obedience, identity as believers, life as strangers in the world, being of one mind); **Ephesians 4:17–5:20** (old and new life, being children of light, being filled with the Spirit).

Day 2 **Read and complete "The Bible Teaching" from "A People Set Apart" through "The Covenant People" in response to your Day 1 reading (pages 98–100). If you have not already completed the spiritual gifts inventory at** *adultbiblestudies.com/ fasttrack***, do so now. Make a note of your top 3–5 spiritual gifts (the first ones listed under the results) on page 108.**

Day 3 **Read Romans 12** (living sacrifice, transformed lives and relationships); **1 Corinthians 12–13** (spiritual gifts, love). **Read "The Bible Teaching" from "Gifts of Each Disciple" through "Biblical Guidance," as well as the "Mark of Discipleship" (pages 100–102).**

Day 4 **Read James 1–2** (standing firm; being doers, not just hearers; God's gifts; showing faith, not favoritism). **Consider what the phrase** *faith without actions is dead* **(2:26) means. Read and complete "The Bible Teaching" under "Spiritual Gifts" on pages 103–107.**

Day 5 **Read James 3-5** (conflict with people and God, warning to the proud and haughty, courageous patience). Consider how, after eleven (or possibly twenty-three) sessions with your group, you have experienced what James 5:13-20 teaches.

Day 6 **Read 1 Corinthians 1:17-31** (human wisdom versus the cross); **John 13:1-20** (foot washing). **Consider the message and the reminder in these two passages. Complete the "Spiritual Gifts Assignment" on pages 108–109. List names of other group members and their gifts you have identified.** *This work is very important to complete and bring to your last session.*

Day 7 **Rest, pray, and attend class.**

DISCIPLE FAST TRACK

THE BIBLE TEACHING

A People Set Apart

Holy means set apart for God. A chalice is set apart for Holy Communion, not used for orange juice at breakfast. A sanctuary is set apart for worship, not used for roller blading on Saturday night. In a secular world, some things are set apart as sacred.

Holy has the same root as words like *whole*, *wholesome*, *holistic*, *heal*, *health*, and *hallow*. To be holy is to be whole, clean, healthy, harmonious.

We learned from the beginning that God called a special people to be set apart, to be different, to be "peculiar." First Peter assumes that the Christian community has now become the "set-apart people," a "peculiar" people.

Baptism

Some scholars think First Peter may have been a baptismal sermon before it became a general letter to the churches of Asia Minor. Baptismal images abound. The words *he has given us new birth . . . born anew into a living hope* (1 Peter 1:3) not only recall our Lord's appeal to Nicodemus (John 3:3) but also Paul's allusion to the death of self and resurrection with Christ in baptism (Romans 6:4). In First Peter, we have a strong emphasis on the new creation in Christ rather than only on a washing away of sin's stain. A baptized Christian is born anew and lives in a new community. Baptism, like circumcision of old, signifies initiation into the corporate life of God's people.

Christian baptism also calls to memory the deliverance in the crossing of the water of the Red Sea and the promise in the walking through the water of the river Jordan.

In an arid country, minimal amounts of water were available. The early church used the scallop shell for baptism and ultimately ruled that three drops of water were minimal for baptism in the name of the Father, the Son, and the Holy Spirit.

When you see a person baptized in the church, in what ways do you believe that person is "set apart"?

Blood

Just as the Hebrews in Egypt sprinkled their doorposts with the blood of the sacrificial lamb (Exodus 12:21-23; 12:5), the holy people (priests and people) were sprinkled with blood (24:8;

29:21), and so later Christians have symbolically been sprinkled with the blood of Christ. "You were liberated by the precious blood of Christ, like that of a flawless, spotless lamb" (1 Peter 1:19). As Christians, we remember the divine sacrifice when we drink the cup of wine in Holy Communion and when we sing songs of God's grace, atonement, and forgiveness. As you think about receiving Holy Communion, in what ways have you understood yourself and others to be "set apart"?

The Covenant People

In the Old Testament, elderly Abraham and Sarah were called to found a "chosen people," to walk out in faith, turning away from idols. They and their offspring formed a covenant community characterized by trust in the one God, rest on the Sabbath, hospitality to strangers, male circumcision, the tithe, family loyalty, and rejection of infant sacrifice. Later the covenant people were commanded to be unusually compassionate with the poor, especially careful with the weak, and never forgetful that they too were once helpless slaves in the land of Egypt (Leviticus 19). With the giving of the Mosaic food laws (Leviticus 11), the covenant people became increasingly "peculiar." Then they were really set apart.

But as we have learned, instead of being humbly set apart for service, the Pharisees of Jesus' day broke hospitality with the world and withdrew into a rigid adherence to the Law that resulted in self-righteous aloofness. They became "holier-than-thou" rather than holy as God is holy. That can happen. Describe how you have seen it happen sometimes to Christians.

First Peter tells us we are to be "a chosen race, a royal priesthood, a holy nation, . . . God's own possession" (1 Peter 2:9). What does that mean? We are called to be holy because *our God is holy*. Notice the descriptions in First Peter of the new Christian community: self-disciplined (1 Peter 1:13); "obedient children," not conformed to "your former desires, those that shaped you when you were ignorant" (1:14); obedient "to the truth," showing "genuine affection for your fellow believers" and loving one another "deeply and earnestly" (1:22). This new holy priesthood of all believers is supposed to rid themselves of "all ill will and all deceit, pretense, envy, and slander" (2:1). As "a holy priesthood" we are to "offer spiritual sacrifices" (2:5), abstaining from "worldly desires" (2:11). We must conduct ourselves to "live honorably among the unbelievers" so that "in the day when God visits to judge they will glorify him, because they have observed your honorable deeds" (2:12). We are to be distinctively honest, humble, and caring.

"Holy people" have an "inner" mark of character and an "outer" mark of compassion. Some things are a "no"-saying: drunkenness, adultery, lying, and the like. Some things are a "yes"-saying: witnessing, practicing hospitality, striving for peace and justice, caring for the broken and the hard-pressed. Holiness, of an arrogant form, usually emphasizes a few "no" rules, ignores others, and entirely forgets sacrificial ministry in the world. When Mother Teresa of India said about her care for the dying, "I do it for Jesus' sake," she caught the spirit of First and Second Peter.

The disciple may wear the same kind of clothes others are wearing, speak the same language, live in the same city; but the disciple is different and knows this must be. Called out of worldly pursuits and careless living, the disciple, like Abraham, is summoned to be a part of a "set-apart" people, blessed to be a blessing.

Think about your own life, about how Christ has helped you be "set apart," yet how much you have to grow to really be a part of the "royal priesthood."

As a disciple of Jesus Christ, part of a "set-apart people," what are some things in this world you need to say "no" to? What are some things you need to say "yes" to?

Gifts of Each Disciple

None of us, not even the ones most committed to Jesus Christ, see ourselves clearly and accurately. That is why we place ourselves under spiritual leaders and in the company of fellow Christians. Often others see our spiritual usefulness more clearly than we see it ourselves.

We have two goals for this session:

1. To *identify*, by ourselves and in the group, our personal talents, our gift to the fellowship.

Mark of Discipleship
Disciples know themselves as distinctive, peculiar people bearing the inner mark of character and the outer mark of compassion, committing their lives completely to God and using their gifts in ministry.

2. To *commit* ourselves, with the encouragement of the group, to serve God in a specific capacity in the days ahead.

Others in the group will be waiting to receive your thoughts about their gifts, trusting your judgment and your spiritual insight. Spend as much time thinking and praying about their gifts as about your own. They too will be ready to decide their specific ministry for the days ahead.

In addition to studying the Bible passages, think about the needs of your congregation and the hurts of the world. Think carefully about children and their needs, about youth and ways to reach them, about adults and their pain. Think of physical, spiritual, financial, and emotional needs of people you know. Think of the least, the last, and the lost; the wealthy and the self-satisfied. Remember the sick, the poor, and people who live without faith or hope. Think of individuals who, like the Samaritan woman, are cut off from the community or discriminated against.

Think of ways you can train others, build others up, guide and direct other disciples to empower the fellowship.

Biblical Guidance

We need to remember some things we have learned. Look up the related Scripture references to refresh your memory:

- God works in unusual, surprising ways to accomplish spiritual tasks. Remember Sarah and Abraham (Genesis 18:9-15).
- Sometimes God uses weakness to show that power belongs to God. Remember what Paul said in 1 Corinthians 1:26-29.
- God can do much through people who willingly turn themselves and what they have over to God. Remember Barnabas, the "son of encouragement" (Acts 4:36-37).
- God does not reveal the divine will to the curious but to the obedient. Remember Peter (John 21:15-19).
- Talent is varied. So are gifts. You are uniquely a part of the body of Christ. No one can take your special place. Remember 1 Corinthians 12:27-31.
- Leadership in the church requires unusual humility and a willingness to serve without glory. Remember Jesus' washing of the disciples' feet (John 13:1-17).
- No one has enough power to achieve spiritual ministry alone. You will need God's help. Copy as your text Philippians 4:13.

How do you determine what your "gifts" are? Older people know through experience what they enjoy, what "they are good at," what others compliment them on, what gives them a sense of satisfaction, what seems to be helpful or useful to other people, and what God seems to be pushing or pulling them to do.

However, even experienced adults are often novices in spiritual ministries and timid about trying new or different work. Vast opportunities for service or unexplored ways of serving are yet untried. Fresh outpourings of the Holy Spirit can make available surprising gifts to older people.

DISCIPLE FAST TRACK

Younger people are often feeling their way. Lacking a great deal of experience, they can try new things—sometimes working alone, sometimes with supervision. Many an excellent teacher began as an assistant. Many disciples are asked to be helpers, then turn into prophets and preachers.

Sometimes persons receive or discover new gifts when they find themselves in new situations. The death of a loved one may show a person to be a healer through the consoling of other family members. Discussion of a social issue with friends may cause someone to respond as a prophet.

Gifts differ from talents. Talents are God-given, natural, a part of the created order. Gifts are received through the Holy Spirit. Both talents and gifts can be used to serve God.

Gifts are also different from the fruit of the Spirit (Galatians 5:22-23). The fruit of the Spirit is for everyone and grows with varying degrees in each disciple. "The fruit of the Spirit is love, joy, peace, patience, kindness, goodness, faithfulness, gentleness, and self-control." Let these qualities grow in you like wildfire.

Gifts are roles or special abilities, different and distinct and achievable through the Holy Spirit. The Spirit distributes these gifts diversely to each disciple. Many are listed in Romans 12 and 1 Corinthians 12, but we will focus on only seven. They are gifts to be apostles, prophets, teachers, workers of miracles, healers, helpers, and administrators (1 Corinthians 12:28-31, RSV). (We discussed speaking in tongues in our study of Corinthians.)

What are some gifts disciples should exhibit (Romans 12)?

What does the analogy between Christ's body and the human body tell me about the purpose of my unique contribution (1 Corinthians 12)?

How can I serve my ministry so that it will confirm to the "more excellent way" (1 Corinthians 12:31, NRSV), the way of love?

Spiritual Gifts
Apostles

This gift is to exercise general oversight and leadership in the church. A person called to apostolic ministry shows signs of spiritual power to lead others to Christ, to encourage, and to build up others in faith and love. Pastors are apostles ordained to preach the word, maintain order, and administer the sacraments. Paul said that he was "called to be an apostle."

Do you feel that you are being called into the full-time apostolic ministry of the church?

Are there persons in the group who exhibit evidence of this gift and who, you believe, are being "called to be an apostle"? Name them.

Prophets

A prophet is one who speaks for God. The spiritual gift is to receive and communicate a message of God to the people. Such disciples may witness quietly in private conversations. They may testify, speak, or preach in public. Some prophets are social activists, writing or speaking a Christlike word on public issues. Some may serve in political life or in community service. Even though they may receive criticism, prophets express a biblical truth in a chaotic, selfish world.

Prophets may focus on exhortation, encouragement, consolation (Isaiah 40:1-2), or on conviction, confrontation, social change (Acts 4:19-20).

As you think about the group, which persons, if any, seem suited to be prophets?

What forms might their ministry take?

Do you have the gift of speaking for God? In what ways might you use that gift?

Teachers

While it is true that not everyone should be a teacher (James 3:1), the church always needs Christlike teachers. Some people who are professionally trained can be inadequate as teachers in the church or can be splendid teachers. Some people who have no formal training are gifted teachers.

Keep in mind the variety of teaching. Some teachers are excellent as lecturers, others as small group discussion leaders.

Jesus is called the great Teacher. He imparted knowledge, but he also trained disciples. Learning and training in the faith go together. Read 1 Timothy 1:3-7. Remember, too, the DISCIPLE study program will grow and touch the lives of countless numbers as some teachers are identified in each group to guide new study groups.

Do you think that God has enabled you to be a teacher in the church?

Do you think that some members of the group are gifted teachers? Name them. (If you identify an age group for which they are uniquely suited, mention that.)

Who in the group could suitably teach DISCIPLE FAST TRACK?

If asked to teach, would you be willing?

Miracle Workers

Some people seem gifted with power to perform miracles, signs, and wonders. Peter's prayer restored Tabitha to life (Acts 9:36-41). Sometimes tormented individuals are released from fear or guilt or grief by people who work wonders. In the early church it was a miracle when Jewish Christians and Gentile Christians sold everything and shared it "as any had need." Many incredible things took place, called "wonders and signs" (2:43-45).

In a group, sometimes gifted people work wonders—speaking a soft word to ease tension, showing a fresh way to overcome an impasse, introducing a new inquirer to grace. Such Christians can serve as lay leaders. Some people pray for others and invite them to come to Christ. Other Christians, with a word, a deed, or a gift, mobilize the whole church for action. They become "miracle workers."

Have you spotted someone in the group who is a worker of miracles?

Healers

Some people walk into a sick room and patients feel better. Countless Christians testify that the prayers of the church helped heal them, sometimes with laying on of hands, receiving Holy Communion, or anointing with oil (James 5:13-16).

Have you ever felt the healing power of God when people were praying for you?

Do not discount professionals. Doctors, nurses, aides, psychologists, social workers, and paramedics can be spiritually gifted as well as technically trained. Some have healing in their hands, their voice, their compassion.

Healing of the soul is the ministry of some. Remember that illnesses can result from unresolved grief, guilt, or unfounded fear. God uses special persons to heal the soul and thereby heal the body.

Healing or reconciliation between persons or groups is a powerful spiritual force. "All of these new things are from God, who reconciled us to himself through Christ and who gave us the ministry of reconciliation" (2 Corinthians 5:18).

Remember also that even people with the gift of healing do not heal every time (2 Corinthians 12:7-9). Healings do not always depend on the sick person's faith or on the faith of the persons praying (John 9:3).

Identify persons in the group who might be healers. The gift of healing is similar to the gift of miracle working, but don't worry. We are not concerned about sharp definitions; we are praying for spiritual power.

Has God used you in the ministry of healing? When?

Might God use you as a healer? How?

Helpers

No gift is more important to the church. "Helping" lubricates the gears, making church life active, abundant, and joyous. To be called "one who encourages" (Acts 4:36) is to be highly praised. The seven Hellenists who took over the feeding of the widows were helpers (Acts 6:2-6).

But be careful. Agreeing to "help" may be ducking responsibility. Help when? Help where? Help whom? How often and how much? A gifted helper says yes even at some sacrifice or inconvenience. Willingness to serve is a precious spiritual gift.

NOTES

Everyone is a helper of sorts. Are you an especially gifted helper? Indicate some places where you could be unusually helpful.

Who in the group stands out as a Barnabas, always willing to help?

Administrators

The gift of administration is the ability God gives to certain members of the body of Christ to establish goals and to devise and execute plans to accomplish those goals. Ability to organize a team; grace to inspire, encourage, and delegate; willingness to hold people accountable with courtesy—these are the talents and gifts of administration.

Many businessmen and businesswomen do not think of themselves as spiritual. Yet they steer the church wisely in matters of planning, finance, building projects, and service and relief programs. The ability to listen, the ability to communicate clearly, and the ability to make decisions are necessary signs of this gift. Jethro helped Moses become a better administrator (Exodus 18:13-26). The Twelve wisely turned the feeding of the widows over to "men . . . well-respected and endowed by the Spirit with exceptional wisdom" (Acts 6:3). Bishops are expected to be good administrators (1 Timothy 3:1-7). A Sunday school superintendent is as important as a teacher.

If a congregation is to work smoothly, some gifted people must organize and administer. Who in your group, including you, is a gifted administrator?

DISCIPLE FAST TRACK

Spiritual Gifts Assignment

After completing the spiritual gifts inventory at *adultbiblestudies.com/fasttrack* and the "Spiritual Gifts" assignment in "The Bible Teaching" section (pages 103–107), complete this page, except for question 2, which you will complete in your final class session. You will use this sheet in your group to share with your group about your gifts and the gifts of others in your group.

1. I feel my spiritual gift(s) are:

2. My group perceives my gift(s) to be:

3. I plan to give myself in a special way this coming year to

4. Below are the seven spiritual gifts you pondered in the "Bible Teaching" section. Write the names of any of your group members that you perceive may have these gifts. (You are not expected to have identified gifts for everyone in your group. You are to record only what you perceived. Others will have additional ideas.)

Apostles:

Prophets:

Teachers:

DISCIPLE or DISCIPLE FAST TRACK teachers:

Miracle workers:

Healers:

Administrators:

TIMELINE OF NEW TESTAMENT BIBLICAL HISTORY

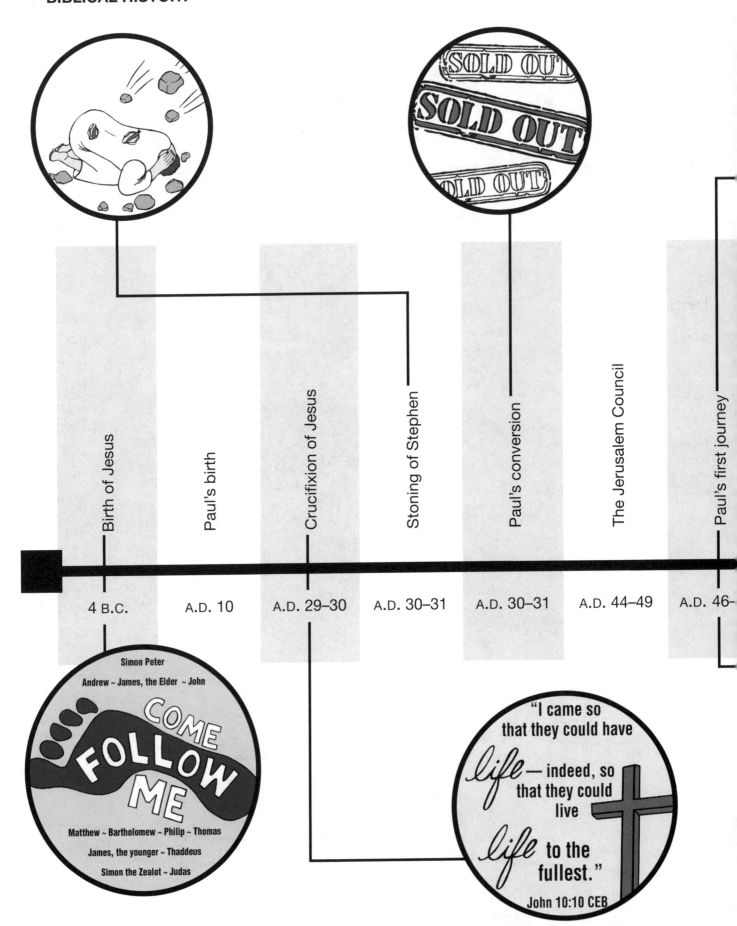

Birth of Jesus

Paul's birth

Crucifixion of Jesus

Stoning of Stephen

Paul's conversion

The Jerusalem Council

Paul's first journey

4 B.C.   A.D. 10   A.D. 29–30   A.D. 30–31   A.D. 30–31   A.D. 44–49   A.D. 46–

SOLD OUT
SOLD OUT
OLD OUT

Simon Peter

Andrew ~ James, the Elder ~ John

COME FOLLOW ME

Matthew ~ Bartholomew ~ Philip ~ Thomas

James, the younger ~ Thaddeus

Simon the Zealot ~ Judas

"I came so that they could have *life*—indeed, so that they could live *life* to the fullest."

John 10:10 CEB

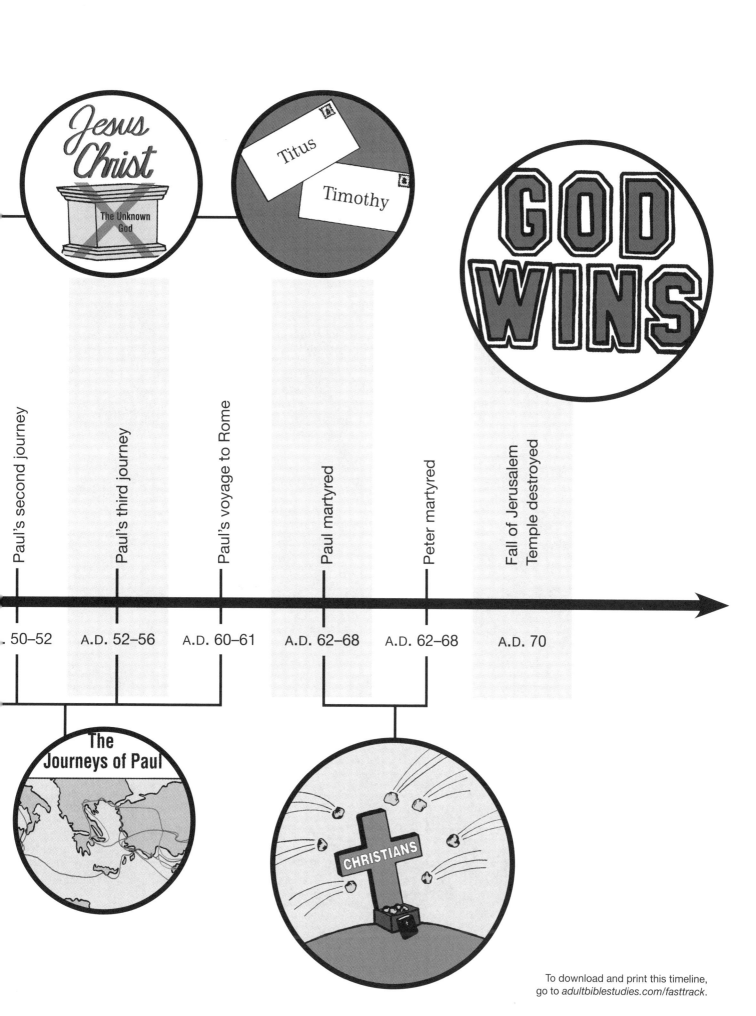

Jesus Christ

The Unknown God

Titus

Timothy

GOD WINS

Paul's second journey

Paul's third journey

Paul's voyage to Rome

Paul martyred

Peter martyred

Fall of Jerusalem Temple destroyed

50–52

A.D. 52–56

A.D. 60–61

A.D. 62–68

A.D. 62–68

A.D. 70

The Journeys of Paul

CHRISTIANS

To download and print this timeline, go to adultbiblestudies.com/fasttrack.